Teaching and Researching Speaking

APPLIED LINGUISTICS IN ACTION

General Editors:

Christopher N. Candlin and David R. Hall

Books published in this series include:

Teaching and Researching Autonomy in Language Learning	Phil Benson
Teaching and Researching Motivation	Zoltán Dörnyei
Teaching and Researching Lexicography	R.R.K. Hartmann
Teaching and Researching Translation	Basil Hatim
Teaching and Researching Speaking	Rebecca Hughes
Teaching and Researching Writing	Ken Hyland
Teaching and Researching Listening	Michael Rost
Teaching and Researching Reading	Willam Grabe and Fredricka L. Stoller

Teaching and Researching Speaking

Rebecca Hughes

An imprint of **Pearson Education**

London · New York · Toronto · Sydney · Tokyo · Singapore · Hong Kong · Cape Town
New Delhi · Madrid · Paris · Amsterdam · Munich · Milan · Stockholm

PEARSON EDUCATION LIMITED

Head Office:
Edinburgh Gate
Harlow CM20 2JE
Tel: +44 (0)1279 623623
Fax: +44 (0)1279 431059

London Office:
128 Long Acre
London WC2E 9AN
Tel: +44 (0)20 7447 2000
Fax: +44 (0)20 7240 5771
Website: www.history-minds.com

_____

First published in Great Britain in 2002

© Pearson Education, 2002

The right of Rebecca Hughes to be identified as Author
of this Work has been asserted by her in accordance
with the Copyright, Designs and Patents Act 1988.

ISBN 0 582 40454 1

British Library Cataloguing in Publication Data
A CIP catalogue record for this book can be obtained from the British Library

Library of Congress Cataloguing in Publication Data
A CIP catalogue record for this book can be obtained from the Library of Congress

10 9 8 7 6 5 4 3 2 1

Set in 10.5/12pt Janson by Graphicraft Limited, Hong Kong
Printed in Malaysia, LSP

The Publishers' policy is to use paper manufactured from sustainable forests.

To my mother, Alyna Hughes

Contents

Acknowledgements   xi

Introduction   1

Section I   Issues in teaching and researching speaking   3

  1   Conceptual and historical background   5

1.1   Introduction   5
1.2   The skill of speaking   6
1.3   The nature of speech in contrast to writing   9
1.4   Where does speech fit in language studies?   15
1.5   Summary   25

  2   The research space: paradigms and problems   27

2.1   Introduction   27
2.2   Classical research paradigms in relation to researching
      speaking   27
2.3   Attitudes to speech data   28
2.4   The applicability of research approaches and frameworks
      to the study of speech   33
2.5   The problem of the status of speech in applied linguistics   35
2.6   Where are the data for research into speech?   36
2.7   Summary   42

Section II   Issues for teaching and assessing speaking   45

3   Approaches, materials and the problem of 'real' speech   47

3.1   Introduction   47
3.2   Spoken interaction in context   49
3.3   Teaching global speaking skills   50
3.4   Teaching spoken grammar   61
3.5   Perspectives on pronunciation and fluency   67
3.6   Bringing the skills together   71
3.7   Summary   71

4   Issues in assessing speaking   73

4.1   Introduction   73
4.2   Language proficiency versus speaking proficiency   76
4.3   The issue of interactivity   78
4.4   The issue of creating authentic conditions for speech testing 79
4.5   The issue of spoken genres and testing   82
4.6   Integrated versus discrete skills testing   83
4.7   A comparison of test paradigms for oral assessment   84
4.8   The criteria for three tests of speaking compared   86
4.9   Summary   88

5   Approaches to researching speech   90

5.1   Introduction   90
5.2   Research into global features of speech   90
5.3   Grammar, structural choices and the spoken language   99
5.4   Research into fluency and pronunciation   108
5.5   Summary   117

6   Some new directions   119

6.1   Introduction   119
6.2   Mode-based research   120
6.3   Theoretical orientations on the role and status of speech 121
6.4   Evidence from speech pathology   124
6.5   Modality, processing and memory   125
6.6   Speaking, writing and teaching spoken/written forms of
       language   126

6.7 Summary of central issues discussed in relation to new
approaches to speech   129
6.8 Summary   130

Section III   Researching speaking   131

7 Classrooms, research and spoken mode   133

7.1 Introduction   134
7.2 Implications of the nature of spoken discourse on
teaching speech   134
7.3 Moving towards your own project on spoken discourse   136
7.4 Sources of inspiration for research   138

8 Research project ideas and frameworks   142

8.1 Introduction   142
8.2 Projects on oral interaction: a discourse analysis approach
and an experimental approach   143
8.3 Projects on one particular spoken discourse feature:
an action-research approach and a conversation analysis
approach   149
8.4 Projects on oral task difficulty: two approaches to
quantifying complexity   153
8.5 Projects on differences between mode: two experimental
approaches   158

Section IV   Resources and further information   165

9 Research borders and boundaries   167

9.1 Introduction   167
9.2 Speaking and ethnographic or cross-cultural studies   168
9.3 Speaking and psycholinguistics   169
9.4 Speaking and neuro-linguistic studies   169
9.5 Speaking and corpus linguistics   169
9.6 Speaking and new technologies   170

10	Research resources	171
10.1	Traditional library resources	171
10.2	Databases and sound archives (both on-line and on CD-ROM)	172
10.3	Speech corpora	173
10.4	Societies and organisations	173
10.5	Speech recognition and text-to-speech	174
10.6	On-line pronunciation and intonation resources	174
10.7	Research skills summaries	174
10.8	Other on-line resources	178

Glossary	180
References	185
Index	194

Acknowledgements

I would like to thank all those who have supported me in the process of writing this book including:

My husband, Kieron O'Hara, who has, as ever, maintained my sanity through his love and good counsel.

My teaching colleagues at the Centre for English Language Education who supported me throughout a challenging two year period for the Centre.

My research colleagues in the School of English Studies, University of Nottingham and most particularly Ronald Carter who first suggested I might like to write this book.

Chris Candlin and David Hall whose supportive and insightful comments aided me throughout the process of writing.

I would like to pass on sincere thanks to the editorial team at Longman.

For all who have helped me in writing this book, my sincere thanks; whatever shortcomings remain should be laid at my door.

The publishers are grateful to the following for permission to reproduce copyright material:

Cambridge University Press for extracts from *Exploring Spoken English* by Ronald Carter and Michael McCarthy, 1997, pp. 64–5; *Study Speaking: A Course in Spoken English for Academic Purposes* by Tony Lynch and Kenneth Anderson, 1992, pp. 24–5; and *Discussions A–Z Intermediate: A Resource Book of Speaking Activities*, 1997, p. 55; Oxford University Press for *Everyday Listening and Speaking* by Sarah Cunningham and Peter Moor © Oxford University Press 1992; Language Teaching Publications for *Conversation Gambits (Real English Conversation Practices)* by Eric Keller and Sylvia T. Warner, 1988, p. 51; and *Partners 3: More Demanding Pair Work Practices* by Michael Lewis, with additional ideas by Margot Richardson and Jimmie Hill, 1982, p. 284; and to Macmillan Education for *Elementary Conversation* by Marion Geddes and Gill Sturtridge, reprinted by permission of Macmillan Education, Oxford.

In some instances we have been unable to trace the owners of copyright material, and we would appreciate any information that would enable us to do so.

Introduction

Who is this book for?

This book is intended for classroom professionals or higher degree students who need to have an up-to-date, detailed, and straightforward summary of current research and issues in the field of teaching and researching speaking. In part, the book aims to assist communication between students and practising teachers on the one hand, and theoreticians and researchers in applied linguistics on the other by helping to position work on the skill of speaking in the context of classroom issues and research perspectives.

In particular, in this book I hope to help the reader to gain enough background knowledge to approach their own research project in the field with greater confidence. Therefore, rather than merely summarising ideas from academic texts and articles I will, from time to time, be trying to relate them to some of the research skills and processes which lie behind them.

A thread through the book which it is hoped will help the reader to 'navigate' is the division of the skill of speaking into three broad areas:

discourse and interactions, discourse and grammar, fluency and pronunciation.

The structure of the book

There are four main sections to this book, each of which addresses key issues in the following areas:

Section I: This gives the background to and context for the present situation in teaching and researching speaking. Here there are two contextualising chapters, the first giving the historical background to research and attitudes to teaching speaking, the second summarising current research into the topic, current paradigms and issues in the field.

Section II: This gives a more detailed description of research applications, assessment and classroom issues. The first of four chapters in the section gives an overview of approaches and materials in the domain of teaching speaking and addresses the issue of how far 'real' speech is dealt with in the classroom. The next chapter deals with the assessment of speech and is followed by a chapter summarising several approaches to researching speech through case-study material. A final, brief, chapter reviews trends in current mode-based research and possible new directions.

Section III: The first chapter in this section returns to the issue of the need for further research into the topic of speech in its own right. The next section provides further case studies and suggestions for a number of research projects capable of being carried out by classroom practitioners or students.

Section IV: The final section gives an overview of cross-disciplinary relationships, and research resources that are available both in traditional media such as print bibliographies and journals, and newer media such as CD Roms and the Internet. There is a glossary of key terms at the end of the section.

I Issues in teaching and researching speaking

Chapter 1

Conceptual and historical background

This chapter will...

- investigate and describe some of the typical features of spoken discourse;
- provide a historical context for the processes and attitudes to teaching and researching speech;
- begin to highlight some of the problems in teaching and researching speaking arising from attitudes to speech which have tended to prevail in linguistic theory.

1.1 Introduction

A central theme which this chapter discusses is the status of speech in society at different points in time, and in linguistic theory and practice in particular. A significant issue which I will be addressing throughout this book is the fact that the spoken form has gained primacy of status in language sciences this century to the point where there has been a merging in applied linguistic, and wider research circles, of the concept of 'speaking' with 'language'.

The chapter tries to explain this process, why it is significant, and why, paradoxically, it has led to a lack of explicit attention within linguistic theory to the faculty of speech in its own right. The conceptual and (brief) historical overviews in this chapter are intended to show some of the implications of this issue for the practice and theory of language teaching.

1.2 The skill of speaking

> **Quote 1.1** An early plea for the teaching of speaking in its own right
>
> With regard indeed to the pronunciation of our tongue, the obstacles are great; and in the present state of things almost insuperable. But all this apparent difficulty arises from our utter neglect of examining and regulating our speech; as nothing has hitherto been done, either by individuals, or societies, towards a right method of teaching it.
>
> (Sheridan, 1781: v–vi)

1.2.1 Speaking is not a discrete skill

One of the central difficulties inherent in the study of speaking is that it overlaps with a considerable number of other areas and activities. How far, for instance, is the structure of a conversation culturally determined? How far is the grammar of speech different from other sorts of grammar? What are the critical factors in the stream of speech which make it intelligible? This book attempts to carve out a niche for speaking in its own right whilst breaking it down into three distinct areas: the global or discourse level, the structural level and the level of speech production.

These three areas broadly relate to fairly stable areas of activity in linguistics of discourse, lexis and grammar, and phonology/phonetics and map on to, and overlap with, other threads of study in theoretical and applied linguistics. Some of the relationships are indicated in Figure 1.1.

1.2.2 Teaching speaking is not easily separated from other objectives

A further complicating factor is that when the spoken language is the focus of classroom activity there are often other aims which the teacher might have: for instance, helping the student to gain awareness of or to practice some aspect of linguistic knowledge (whether a grammatical rule, or application of a phonemic regularity to which they have been introduced), or to develop production skills (for example rhythm, intonation or vowel-to-vowel linking), or to raise awareness of some socio-linguistic or pragmatic point (for instance how to interrupt politely, respond to a compliment appropriately, or show that one has understood).

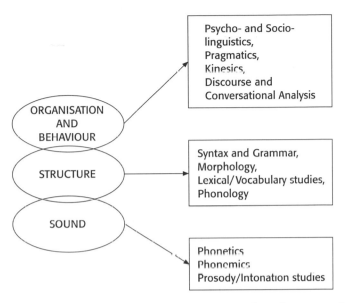

Figure 1.1   **Levels and fields of research into speech and conversation**

1.2.3   Teaching speaking versus using speaking to teach

A key question to ask, therefore, is whether a teacher is engaged in 'teaching the spoken form of a language' or 'teaching a language through speaking'. This distinction is important although it may seem trivial at first sight. Spoken forms of language have been under-researched whether at the level of grammar or in broader genre based studies. I will be arguing that this is due, in part, to attitudes to language data in linguistic theory. Whereas a teacher or materials writer may feel some confidence in dealing with stable written forms and genres – the essay, the business letter, the laboratory report – and have some feel for the language appropriate to newer discourses – such as e-mail – the notion of how spoken genres are structured and what forms are most typical of them is difficult to establish. I will also be suggesting that this means there is a great deal of speaking going on in classrooms, but that this is different from 'teaching speaking'.

1.2.4   Insights from speech corpora

The objectives in the speaking classroom may well change quite radically over the next ten years as insights emerging from corpora of natural speech and language processing combine to help us understand what speaking is actually like.

Concept 1.1   **Corpus/corpora (pl.)/corpus linguistics**

At its most simple, a corpus (in linguistic contexts) is a collection of language samples. As such, a teacher's collection of photocopies of student essays might be regarded as a corpus. However, the term is strongly associated with the computer-aided analysis of language, and, in corpus linguistics, with the statistical analysis of word (and less often) structural frequencies. Just as the teacher might look through a collection of learners' essays before planning a class to see what common problems they were encountering, a corpus linguist can find patterns and frequencies in many million word samples of language. The collection of speech data for corpus design is a particular problem as large amounts of naturally occurring speech need to be both recorded and transcribed for the computer. This is a time-consuming (and expensive!) process and means that there has been a tendency for corpora to be biased in favour of the written mode.

Quote 1.2   The authors of the *Longman Grammar of Spoken and Written English* on findings about speech which run counter to expectations

In many respects, the patterns of use described in the LGSWE will be surprising to materials writers, since they run directly counter to the patterns often found in ESL/EFL coursebooks. For example, progressive aspect verbs are the norm in most books that teach English conversation, in marked contrast to the language produced by speakers in actual conversation, where simple aspect verbs are more than 20 times more common than progressive aspect verbs. Similarly, most ESP/EAP instructors will be surprised to learn that modal verbs are much more common in conversation than in academic prose: in fact, only the modal *may* is used much more commonly in academic prose.

(Biber *et al.*, 1999: 46)

1.2.5   Bringing the facets of speaking together

The human voice and the faculty of speech are inherently bound up with the projection of the self into the world. As a living language is acquired by a second language learner, a large number of other things also need to be adjusted for successful communication to take place. These are matters to do with culture, social interaction, and the politeness norms which exist in the target language. To learn to communicate expertly in another language a speaker must change and expand identity as he or she learns the cultural, social, and even political factors, which go into language choices,

> **Quote 1.3** The authors of the *Cambridge Advanced Grammar of English* on what speech data can tell us about a word which is generally described as a preposition
>
> *Like* is very commonly used in informal spoken English. One of its most frequent uses is as a marker of reported speech, especially where the report involves a personal reaction or response.
> *So this bloke, he was drunk, came up to me and I'm **like** Go away, I don't want to dance.*
>
> ...
> One of the most frequent uses of *like* in spoken English is to focus attention, usually by giving or requesting an example.
> *The first thing that runs through your mind is **like** meningitis, isn't it?*
>
> (Carter and McCarthy, forthcoming)

needed to speak appropriately with a new 'voice'. Therefore, while this book treats the different 'layers' of speaking – discourse, grammar, and phonology – separately, for the purposes of analysis, and, I hope, to clarify them, an underlying theme is that the teacher will ultimately need to help the student bring all these elements together into a new, unified, and appropriate means of communication on the journey from beginner to fluent speaker of another language.

1.3   The nature of speech in contrast to writing

Figures 1.2 and 1.3 provide a visual summary of some of the major, very general contrasts between the spoken and the written forms of language. Further information about the written form aimed at a similar audience to this book can be found in *Teaching and Researching Writing* (Hyland, 2002). The first diagram represents aspects which relate to how the two forms are generated: 'Aspects of Production' and the second deals with tendencies in attitudes to the two forms: 'Social Aspects'.

1.3.1   How speech reaches the world

When speech is considered in opposition to writing, several distinctive features become evident, particularly if the way it is produced is taken as the starting point (see Figure 1.2). Many of these features also affect the skill of listening, dealt with more fully in *Teaching and Researching Listening* (Rost, 2002).

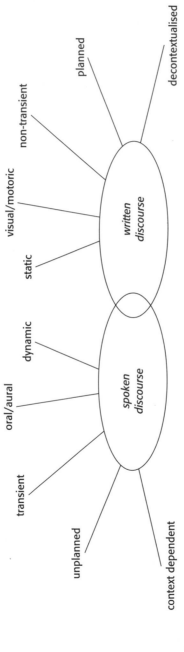

Figure 1.2 Aspects of production

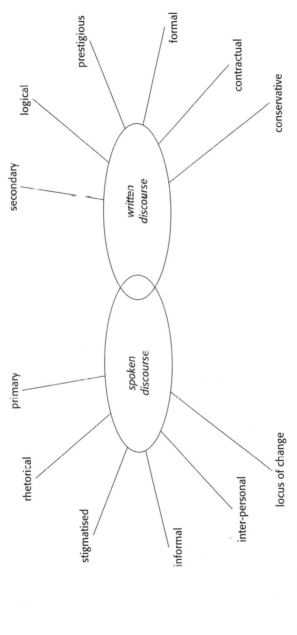

Figure 1.3 Social aspects

Most important, and generally least considered in a linguistic science dominated by texts and recording of texts, is the fact that the spoken form of any language is fundamentally transient. When a word is spoken this event happens within the 'co-ordinates' of a particular place and moment and these can never be reduplicated, although we can now record the word via several different media.

A second, related, factor underpinning the nature of speech, and affecting the type of language choices which can be made, is its delivery via the oral/aural channel.

Concept 1.2   **Channel**

A term used to describe the specific means by which communication takes place. In terms of speaking there is the aural/oral channel and in terms of writing the visual/motoric channel.

Whether in face-to-face situations or via televisual or other media, language which is spoken to be heard is (or should be) quite different from texts created to be read. One of the commonest problems in oral presentations is information overload for listeners as they try to process densely informative language which has been prepared via a written text. Several

Quote 1.4   Chafe and Danielewicz on vocabulary choices in speech as opposed to writing

Choosing lexical items is partly a matter of choosing aptly and explicitly, partly a matter of choosing the appropriate level. In the first case, the deliberateness and editability inherent in writing lead to a more richly varied, less hedged, and more explicit use of words. Speakers are so strongly constrained by their need to produce language rapidly and by their inability to edit, that they are unable to imitate the lexical richness and explicitness of writing even when, as in lecturing, such qualities would be especially valued. In the second case, although the separate histories of spoken and written language have led to partially divergent vocabularies, it is not as hard for speakers to borrow liberally from the written lexicon, or conversely for writers to borrow from the spoken. Thus lectures that are more literary than conversations, and letters more conversational that academic papers. The constraints are not imposed by cognitive limitations, but by judgements of appropriateness.

(Chafe and Danielewicz, 1987: 94)

studies have shown that speakers 'package' their information differently from writers whether at the level of the clause or through vocabulary choices (Biber, 1988; Chafe and Danielewicz, 1987) and subsequent chapters will look at these features in more detail.

Further salient aspects of the way speech is produced again relate to the transient and situated nature of the spoken channel. The vast bulk of spoken material is spontaneous, face-to-face, informal conversation. This kind of discourse is generally unplanned, dynamic and context dependent. A conversation may be guided by one speaker or another who wishes to deal with a particular topic; however, the vagaries of real-time contexts mean that most speech takes the form of a give and take, not only between speakers but also between the discourse and what is happening around it. The type of interesting study which can arise from this is how topics and topic change are managed by speakers, how speakers accommodate themselves to one another, how misunderstandings between speakers are 'repaired', how activity affects language produced, or how reference is made to new/old information within a conversation.

Concept 1.3   **Language in action genres**

This is a type of speech genre which has been under-investigated until recently. Unlike other speech genres, such as narrative, this speech goes on between people who are involved in carrying out a non-linguistic activity, for example, cooking or building furniture. Because the speakers are involved in a task about which they know quite a bit already, there tends to be a high incidence of inexplicit pronominal reference, for example to objects in the sight of all speakers.

1.3.2   How speech is regarded

Figure 1.3 summarises some of the typical attitudes to speech, particularly as it is regarded in literate societies where the function of spoken and written forms are generally clearly demarcated.

Although some theorists, for example Vachek (1973), have argued that the written form of language should be regarded as a separate and wholly independent language system, the spoken form has generally been regarded as the primary form of language upon which the written form is essentially dependent.

One of the essential reasons for this is that in the absence of a pathological reason to prevent it, all humans develop the capacity for speech and it is only later in literate societies (and in the history of humankind) that

> **Quotes 1.5 and 1.6** Two different views of the 'transferability' of speech into writing
>
> It may sometimes happen that an utterance primarily intended for listening needs reading, and vice versa.... In such cases...transposition from the one into the other material is not done with the intention of expressing the given content by means of the other material; if it were so, the only possible accomplishment of the task would be to replace the spoken utterance with the written one or vice versa.
>
> (Vacheck, 1966: 154)
>
> If a text is unintelligible when read aloud, it will also be unintelligible in writing, since the writing merely symbolises the spoken expression.
>
> (Halliday, 1989: 44)

the skill of writing develops. Hence, in Figure 1.3 the indication 'primary' versus 'secondary' for the spoken and written forms.

This is not the place to debate at length the issue of the relative positions of the two forms in linguistic study, however it is important to understand that the innate, universal human capacity for speech has led to its being regarded as the central form of interest to linguists. Therefore, even when theorists appear to pay no attention to actual instances of speech, fundamentally they are pursuing questions to do with the primary language faculty, and this faculty is the universal linguistic form, that is to say, speech.

Ironically, however, although the spoken form takes pride of place in linguistic theory, its status is more ambiguous in society in general. The nature of and, therefore, the functions to which written language is put (most significantly its use as the medium of the binding contract and other legal functions) mean that it is generally held in higher esteem in literate society than the spoken form.

Speech is also quintessentially the form in which the inter-personal functions of language are carried out and the form is subject to the benefits and disadvantages which stem from the way it is produced, as detailed above and summarised in Figure 1.3. Therefore, whereas the tangible, non-ephemeral nature of writing lends it to logical and contractual functions in society, for example record keeping and legal tasks, the spoken form, being essentially more dependent on the time and place it is produced, is used for more informal or rhetorically based tasks. While a powerful political speaker can sway an audience by oratorical devices in debate, it is the written Act of Parliament which can be scrutinised and redrafted which eventually becomes law. And, while you can be known to all your friends by a name quite different from the name on your passport, to change your name on this written document you must engage in an extensive legal process.

Finally, but of very great importance in terms of language change, there is the fact that the spoken form of a language tends to be the laboratory for linguistic innovation. New linguistic items, words and, less quickly, grammatical features tend to be generated in the spoken, rather than the written form of a language, as speakers accommodate their language behaviour to one another and fashions of speaking come and go. As new media such as text messaging on mobile phones, internet chat rooms, e-mail and other electronically delivered forms of writing emerge, this distinction between the speed of innovation in the aural/oral and the visual/motoric channels will become increasingly blurred. However, it is in the deeply interactive forms of language, where people affect one another's language judgements as they communicate in ways which are less restricted by stable, widely accepted conventions, that rapid alterations to language can take place. Despite new media (and in fact because of them in the case of mobile telephony) speech remains the most important locus of change in a language.

To sum up, when speech is looked at both in terms of how it is produced and how it is regarded some of the paradoxes and difficulties involved in studying it come to the fore. This is particularly true when the form is looked at in comparison with the written. For the teacher and for the researcher the dynamic, ever-changing, inter-personally oriented and contextually defined nature of speech can be both a benefit and a drawback.

1.4   Where does speech fit in language studies?

I suggested above that there has tended to be a collapsing together in the discipline of linguistics of the concepts 'language faculty' and the 'faculty of speech'. This in turn has clear repercussions on what comes under the scope of 'research into speaking' at the current time. For if language and speech are seen as the same thing one kind of research will be carried out, and if they are regarded as distinct areas for investigation then different kinds of research will be seen as appropriate.

One of the keystones underlying this issue is the paradigm set out by Noam Chomsky in the 1960s and which in turn has underpinned the greater part of second language acquisition studies, advances in grammatical models, and computer programming in which a linguistic element is required. A central aspect to the discussion of speech is the dichotomy between the language faculty ('competence') and the way language is used in actual speech or writing ('performance'). Essentially, this division stemmed from Chomsky's questioning of how children can master language, and master it in such a way that, eventually, any speaker of a language can create and understand an infinite amount of discourse, most of it entirely new.

Concept 1.4   Competence

Human beings do not have infinite brain power and cannot simply learn and process each new example of language afresh. Therefore, Chomsky suggested an underlying, more basic, language capacity which could generate infinite sentences but was itself pared down enough to be within finite human abilities. This language faculty is what is referred to as 'competence'. Competence, the innate language potentials which all babies seem to be born with, contrasts with the samples of language which any individual baby might hear. Debate continues about the role of input in language acquisition, but, in terms of theory, the peculiarities of any particular speaker, sample of speech, or actual instantiation of a phoneme are categorised as 'performance'. Performance, it is argued, since it is open to the vagaries of individuals, is not really very useful to language theorists. Therefore, in one sense, speech data have no place in 'pure' language science which is more interested in finding out about the nature of competence.

Concept 1.5   Rationalism and empiricism in linguistics

Rationalist and empiricist schools of thought are generally described in contrast to one another. As an empirical approach to something values real-world data a linguist of this persuasion takes it as fundamental that samples of language and 'Language' are inextricably linked. A rationalist, on the other hand, would suggest that we must look inside the brain or the mind in order to investigate 'Language' and that examples of data from the real world are unhelpful and even misleading. The strong influence of the rationalist approach has clear implications for the study of the spoken form as it has tended to move the debate towards idealised and decontextualised examples which in turn fit better with the norms of writing than of speech.

The notion that humans have an innate, more recently articulated as a biological or genetic, language ability, which provides the basis for all language use no matter how seemingly diverse, developed in the twentieth century in opposition to earlier behaviourist models. These two opposing camps, one based on the notion of an innate cognitive model which sees the human child as 'pre-programmed' at birth to learn to speak, the other seeing learning as wholly dependent on an external stimulus, have a strong bearing on both the status of speech data in linguistic science and on theories of teaching language. The second half of this century has seen the rationalist camp win the theoretical battle.

The rationalist model grew from a dissatisfaction with the highly situated nature of earlier behaviourist explanations which relied entirely upon tangible, quantifiable data for input. The rationalist paradigm placed greater store on the logic of the underlying abstract system than on data, and particularly speech data.

Concept 1.6   **Behaviourism**

This concept is strongly associated with the American psychologist B. F. Skinner (1904–1990). The philosophy behind behaviourist models is that learning takes place through interaction with the world – through exposure to examples, through positive and negative stimuli, and trial and error – rather than from any inner faculty.

A great number of the important current issues, therefore, in the science of language relate to how much a researcher believes that the language system can usefully be abstracted away from the situatedness of speech described in previous sections. For example, in universal grammar studies or second language acquisition work a fundamental assumption is that it is not only acceptable, but necessary to ignore most of the vagaries of real speech data (performance) in order to investigate more significant underlying inherent language faculties (competence). A group of language learner's speech in the target language may be analysed for patterns of grammatical use and mis-use, but this will be investigated to provide evidence as to the state of their underlying linguistic knowledge.

At the other end of the spectrum, researchers in the fields of conversation or discourse analysis deal in the actual texture and dynamics of speech (generally through written transcripts, however) looking at how language is delivered and how linguistic and paralinguistic mechanisms, for example eye-contact, pausing or laughter, affect communication. Again, the findings of a particular study will be related to generalisations beyond the limitations of the data analysed, but scholars on this side of the discipline do not in general attempt to link their conclusions to an inherent mental capacity. In these fields there can be seen a swing of the pendulum in recent decades back towards a greater faith in data and against rationalist models.

It can be seen from the brief description of rationally versus empirically based approaches to language study (of which Chomskian rationalism and empirically grounded methods such as discourse and conversation analysis have been presented at each end of the spectrum) that the latter will have

---

Concept 1.7   **Conversation analysis**

Conversation analysis is a branch of linguistics which investigates the structure and social significance of patterns within conversational data. Conversation analysis shares many features with discourse analysis in that both are interested in structures beyond sentence level and the way stretches of language cohere and relate to one another. However, whereas discourse analysis, in its early forms at least, is concerned with 'rule-like' constraints on patterns of turns in conversation, conversation analysis tends to be more purely descriptive in nature.

Concept 1.8   **Discourse analysis**

Many influential ways of looking at language, for example, syntax, regard it as made up of sentences or clauses and investigate the relations between words inside these elements. Discourse analysis, however, is not interested in the relations between items at this level. Rather it looks beyond the sentence or the clause to see what patterns exist between longer sections of conversation or text. For instance, the pair of sentences, 'Good morning, it's a lovely day!' and 'Good bye, see you later!' are individually well-formed, but taken together are rather strange if functioning as an opening and response. Discourse analysts are interested in what constraints there may be on pairs of exchanges, in the typical patterns of initiation and response, or the organisation of talk more generally.

---

more direct and immediate relevance to studies of speech than the former. If a researcher does not believe that actual examples of speech (or writing) provide a sound basis for reaching conclusions about language, they will not give very much consideration to spoken data for their own sake.

However, recent studies have been beginning to question the scope and role of performance data. For example, Berg (1997) takes production errors in speech and in writing as the basis for an investigation of underlying regularities in the language system and in so doing moves from data towards theory. Equally in the realm of data-driven linguistic research the growth of large corpora of the spoken word together with advances in the technology of storing and analysing corpora of speech data mean that there is a growing potential for generalisable conclusions to be made about patterns of speech and speech behaviour. In time, and with a growth of coherent research projects being carried out on them, these corpus-based generalisations may come to match the theoretically elegant conclusions of rationalist frameworks. Finally, cognitive and neuro-linguistic approaches are also pointing up fascinating insights about the processing demands of the spoken and written forms of a language.

1.4.1   Historical perspectives on speaking

The divisions between researchers who rely more heavily on data, and those who treat them with some suspicion did not spring into being in the middle of the twentieth century. Attitudes to the spoken form of language and its position in the curriculum have varied considerably through time, and in different cultures. The germ of the debate can be seen in classical philosophy and attitudes to rhetoric described below.

Furthermore, the status which is given to the faculty of speech in a particular society, or at a particular point in its history, is reflected in the position and emphasis placed on teaching the skill of speaking in the curriculum   something which is as true today as it was in earlier centuries. By looking at how the teaching and study of speech has varied through time a clearer perspective can be gained on how present attitudes fit into a bigger picture, and may point to the ways in which attitudes will change in future.

Attitudes to the spoken form of language have waxed and waned since earliest available records of how and why speaking was taught. These attitudes are usually linked to the ephemeral nature of speech production, and, the fact that until very recently in the history of humanity, spoken language was directed at a present audience by a physically present speaker. In these key facts lie the strengths and weaknesses of the spoken form. On the one hand, its nature permits a speaker to convince, persuade, argue, cajole using all the benefits of being physically in view of the listener through gesture, intonation, eye contact and so on. On the other, unless captured and recorded in some form, the spoken word is fundamentally transient in nature and cannot be checked or scrutinised after the event.

Whereas today the pedagogy of the spoken form tends to be overlooked in favour of the more stable and generally manageable written form the following brief survey shows that at various times great emphasis has been placed on the teaching of speech.

1.4.2   Early attitudes to speech

As far back as Ancient Egypt the art of speaking has been connected to the skill of persuasion, and the ability to influence others by means of rhetoric. One of the earliest extended examples of written language is a papyrus containing advice on the topic of public speaking and disputation for an up-and-coming Egyptian politico: *The Instruction of Ptah-ho-tep and the Instruction of Kegemni* (Gunn, 1918).

With the ancient Greeks the systematisation of argument through speech began with Zeno of Elea (early in the fifth century BC) and reached its height in the teachings of Corax of Syracuse (around 460 BC), and the Sophists. Again, rather than learning the skill of speaking for its own sake, to improve one's own language or for any high-minded pedagogic object-ive, the impetus for this formalisation was a practical and pressing need to argue one's case at law.

Given the strong link between the spoken form and the Sophists it is perhaps interesting that the word 'sophistry' has come to have the negat-ive meaning it now has. The modern meaning of a deliberate use of false or misleading reasoning arose from the attack on the successful teaching of speaking techniques (or rhetorical tricks and devices) by higher-minded philosophers, most notably Plato. In the history of ideas Plato has strong links with arguments based on idealised abstraction which in turn link up with a great deal of modern linguistic theory-driven approaches.

Yet, away from the arena of law and individuals' disputation, the art of speaking continued to influence the history of the nation in major ways as central players in political life (most famously Demosthenes who remained synonymous with oratory and on the curriculum right through to the Renaissance), combined powerful speech making with influential positions in public life. The most extensive 'textbook' to come down to us on the art of speaking at this time is Aristotle's *Rhetoric*, in which the teaching of speaking is divided into notions of the speaker, the audience and the matter of the speech. A great strength of this text was that it managed to synthesise theory and application and, to some extent, bring together the two sides in the style versus content, tricks of delivery versus serious seeking after truth argument which had held since Plato's attack on the Sophists.

The early Greek teachers of the art of speaking introduced key concepts which still underpin Western modes of disputation, such as the persuasive device of arguing from probability, the systematic structuring of speeches, and the art of swaying an audience through emotional appeal. However, the backlash against the spoken form as superficial, transient and open to the ability of individuals to twist listeners' opinions through rhetorical devices reflects more closely the undercurrent of denigration which the spoken form has tended to suffer from, particularly where it exists side-by-side with a more prestigious written form.

With the rise of Roman civilisation and scholars, for example Cicero (106–143 BC) and, later, Quintilian (35–post 96), the theories of oratory of the Greeks were put to consistent, practical use in law and the political arena. However, the debate between the critics of empty rhetoric and proponents of oratory continued. Cicero did much to bridge the gap by emphasising both the need for appeal to the emotions, the sense of humour, and the ear of the listener, together with a deep and detailed understanding of the content being delivered. On the pragmatic side, he preferred to speak last in any debate so that his could be the final appeal to the emotions of the listeners and he studied what particular combinations of phrases, rhythms and cadences were most effective in swaying the audience. However, in *De Oratore* he noted that the truly persuasive speaker needs to have an exceptional grasp of the topic, and that a good general education is the best starting point for a good speaker. Quintilian continued this tradition and was famous as an educator and his *Instituto Oratoria* provides a coherent teaching manual, placing great emphasis on the needs of the individual student.

Interestingly, in the later Rome the need for individuals to routinely plead their own case at law declined, and with the work of Quintilian the emphasis shifts from the use of speech education to meet social and legal needs towards the teaching of rhetoric as an end in itself, and a valuable educational tool to allow individuals to reach their full potential.

It is in this change of emphasis from the teaching of speech as the basis of rhetorical devices towards speech as an educational adjunct that some of the subsequent influence of the classical tradition in Europe can be seen. The legacy of classical attitudes to speech in the Middle Ages and beyond was largely felt within the educational, and initially religious, context. An early solution to the style versus content problem was the splitting up of the teaching programme into different areas, such as grammar (looking at the history and structure of language), logic (the arrangement of thoughts) and rhetoric which at this later stage came to be limited to the delivery of the thoughts. This in turn led in Elizabethan England and wider Renaissance Europe to a tendency for an emphasis on language ornamentation for its own sake, quite divorced from any other educational or social need.

In classical attitudes to teaching speech several issues which remain pertinent today have their roots – for example:

• the relationship between speech and content,
• the role of training versus the natural acquisition of speech,
• the position of speech in the curriculum,
• the influence of differences between individuals on speaking ability.

1.4.3 The eighteenth century and beyond

The following sections continue the historical thread, but look at some of these issues in the narrower context of language teaching as opposed to rhetoric or oratory.

> **Quote 1.7** Howatt on the teaching of speech and social status in eighteenth-century Britain
>
> While the emphasis on correct grammar was even more pronounced in the eighteenth century, the promotion of 'good speech' was another expression of the same passion for accuracy of expression and stylistic elegance. There was considerable popular enthusiasm for instruction in the arts of 'polite conversation', public speaking, and elocution. Out-of-work actors and others with similar gifts had a field-day among the socially ambitious upper-middle classes, particularly in cities anxious to impress the metropolis with their accomplishments. . . .
>
> In spite of this interest in spoken language, it remained essentially 'extra-curricular' and made little impact on the basic education system.
>
> (Howatt, 1985: 76–77)

The beginning and end of the nineteenth century show a marked change in the status of speech in the language teaching process. This was brought about in the transition from 'grammar translation' methods which dominated language teaching in the early parts of the century in Europe to what came to be termed the 'Reform Movement' which arose around the 1880s.

Concept 1.9   **Grammar translation methods**

Although initially intended to simplify the language learning process and widen it from classical Greek and Latin, which had dominated the curriculum, these methods have come to be associated with all that current theories of language teaching abhor: a strong focus on isolated sentences, mechanical translation of sentences in and out of mother tongue, arcane and overly complex grammatical explanation, no place for real (spoken or written) communication.

Concept 1.10   **'Natural' or 'direct' methods**

Partly as a reaction to the 'grammar translation' approach, language teaching reformers at the end of the nineteenth and beginning of the twentieth century argued for a more natural approach to the teaching process. Critically in terms of the interest of this book, they placed the spoken form at the forefront of their pedagogy, generally insisting on mono-lingual speech-based interactions between student and teacher and focusing on matters arising from prompts in the learning context. At its most extreme the 'natural' or 'direct' methods led to 'total physical response' or 'TPR' approaches. In this the student responds through action to instructions given by the teacher in the target language. Fundamental to all the approaches is the primacy of speech, together with a move away from isolated sentences towards meaningful whole texts or interactions.

In the situational (and later functional) and audio-lingual methods developed later in the twentieth century, aided by the improvements in both colour publishing and tape technology, the emphasis on teaching and learning a language through the medium of speech remained at the heart of most teaching methodologies. However, it should be noted that although speech was used in these 'naturally' oriented teaching processes the actual forms used were very far from natural occurring speech or indeed natural spoken communication. Typically, the interactions were highly constrained so that particular grammatical structures could be practised. Such structures were derived from standard formal grammars which were grounded in the norms of 'literate' writing.

Therefore, speech held a paradoxical status in language teaching through the first half of the twentieth century. The notion of 'speaking well' had dominated attitudes to the form from the very earliest teaching traditions associated with it, as noted in previous sections. The grammar translation methods which held sway through much of the nineteenth century were strongly associated with the written form and it was partly as a reaction to this that later movements adopted the oral medium with such enthusiasm. Nonetheless, the return to speech as the primary medium of instruction began a process which remains largely unresolved, that is to say, the simultaneous high regard for the spoken form and the lack of precise attention to the structure and peculiarities of this form in its own right.

The 1960s with the influence of the work of Noam Chomsky, and the 1970s and 1980s with the growth of 'communicative' approaches marked two distinct 'sea-changes' in the field of language teaching both of which did much to underpin present attitudes to the spoken form. While these two threads are, to an extent, brought into commonality by research in the field of second language acquisition they have marked differences in the emphasis they placed on speech in their thinking. On the one hand, the transformational grammar movement internalised and made abstract the language system to such an extent that actual speech became something of an irrelevance. On the other, the tenets of the communicative movement held that language was acquired by meaningful and interesting communication in contexts which mimicked real communicative settings as closely as possible. Thus, for the latter school of thought to conceptualise speech as either simply the medium of instruction (as was the case with natural or direct methods) or as something largely irrelevant to the process of language study (as in the competence/performance distinction) was anathema. At its most extreme, the communicative approach sees the struggle to make and share meaning through the dynamic spoken form the very engine of language acquisition. Nonetheless, the role of mode and the status of speech in language acquisition paradigms has been remarkably undertheorised.

Concept 1.11   Communicative approaches

Due to its wide and deep influence on the field of English language teaching, one often hears about the 'communicative approach'. However, it is perhaps useful to think of a variety of approaches which have changed and developed since the late 1970s in the UK and the USA but all of which share common ground and ideology. Communicative approaches have been strongly associated with the work of Stephen Krashen in the USA on second language acquisition and, among others, Henry Widdowson in the UK. In particular communicative approaches:

- place high value on language in use (as opposed to abstract, isolated examples);
- assert that effective language acquisition (often opposed to language learning) only takes place through language use;
- aim to foster and develop the learner's communicative competence (as opposed to the more abstract concept of linguistic competence);
- regard errors as a natural part of the progression towards a greater understanding of the target language;
- link teaching methodologies to appropriate communicative tasks (rather than seeing classroom tasks as a means of practising a particular grammatical feature)
- tend to favour inductive, student-centred routes to understanding (rather than explicit, teacher-led explanations);
- place the learner at the centre of the learning process and assess progress in relation to factors affecting the individual (for example, levels of motivation).

The basic methods (for example, pair and group work) and beliefs (for instance that teachers should be facilitators of communication tasks rather than dominant 'lecturers' to students) of communicative language teaching have become the backbone of modern English language teaching since the 1970s. Task-based learning, the language awareness movement in the UK and the focus on form movement in America are all later responses to these fundamental tenets.

1.5 Summary

To sum up, this chapter aimed to place the teaching and research of speaking into a conceptual context. In so doing, it drew attention to a fundamental issue in dealing with speech data: the status of instances of real speech within current theories of language, and in particular in the dominant research paradigm behind second language acquisition. The tendency to split off 'pure' linguistic theory from more descriptively or pedagogically oriented studies was discussed. I argued that this is due to the fact that, generally speaking, linguistic theory gives little weight to the activity of speaking itself.

In this chapter the threads of today's issues for teaching and researching speaking were also traced back to classical concerns with the division of form and content in the teaching of speech, and the long shadow cast by these ideas was described. In the concluding section the issue of the status of speech in dominant second language teaching paradigms was noted. Within this section I argued that there has been a tendency for speech to be both highly valued in the modern language teaching contexts and at the same time under-theorised and under-investigated as a faculty in its own right.

Further reading

A succinct history of teaching methods and a balanced discussion of communicative approaches can be found in Chapter 4 of:

Brown, H. D. (1994). *Teaching by Principles: an interactive approach to language pedagogy*. Englewood Cliffs, NJ: Prentice Hall Regents.

A clear introduction to the main features of spoken discourse and their implications for the classroom (with a functional/systemic linguistics bent) can be found in:

Burns, A. and Joyce, H. (1997). *Focus on Speaking*. Sydney: National Center for English Language Teaching and Research, Macquarie University.

A clear introductory but academic and research based outline of some major points of contrast between speech and writing can be read in:

Chafe, W. and Danielewicz, J. (1987). Properties of spoken and written language. In R. Horowitz and S. J. Samuels (Eds), *Comprehending Oral and Written Language*. San Diego, CA: Academic Press, pp. 83–113.

A good overview of Universal Grammar, and which has been revised to incorporate newer ideas on the topic is:

Cook, V. and Newson, M. (1996). *Chomsky's Universal Grammar: an introduction*. Oxford: Blackwell.

Further discussion of the theoretical implications of the differences between speech and writing can be found in Chapter 6 of:

Hughes, R. (1996). *English in Speech and Writing: investigating language and literature.* London: Routledge.

Further discussion of the relationship between speech data and language teaching can be found in:

McCarthy, M. (1998). *Spoken Language and Applied Linguistics.* Cambridge: Cambridge University Press.

Chapter 2

The research space: paradigms and problems

This chapter will . . .

- describe some classical research paradigms as they relate to speaking and spoken data;
- discuss particular problems and issues surrounding research into speaking;
- discuss the role and status of spoken data in language theory.

2.1 Introduction

This chapter begins with a brief look at research paradigms in general, and the usefulness and applicability of these in relation to researching speaking are then considered. I also address the question of where the data for research into speech lie, together with the central issue in researching speaking: the role of inherent psychological faculties as opposed to external, contextual or motivational factors. Finally, there is a brief section on the links between the research issues and classroom concerns.

2.2 Classical research paradigms in relation to researching speaking

While a variety of research methods are represented in the articles described in the following chapters, the research approaches dealt with in this book are, in general, empirically based. That is to say they deal in real-world data of some kind – systematically recorded observations of classroom behaviour, transcripts of conversation, recordings of learners' utterances analysed for particular phonemes and so on. These data are generally gathered to investigate a central research question, often posed as a hypothesis, and are used as the basis of either a quantitative analysis (most often) or a qualitative analysis (less frequent apart from areas such as critical linguistics, socio-linguistics and ethnographically based work).

A major type of approach, which is usually presented in contrast to the empirical ones largely dealt with in this book, is the theoretical approach. Here the researcher is more interested in models, high-level concepts, the relationships between previous theories and new ones, or abstractions in general than any real-world data. Indeed, in the context of extremely theoretically oriented work, for example philosophical logic (a discipline with a surprising amount of influence on linguistics), any real-world data are, if they are considered at all, seen as 'messy', subject to the vagaries of individual circumstances and irrelevant.

Different disciplines will place different emphasis on the role of theory versus data, and in linguistics (and thus applied linguistics) the relationship is particularly complex. Partly because of the high value placed on work which deals first and foremost in abstraction rather than drawing on extensive real-world examples any new academic discipline will tend to feel more comfortable if it adopts the constructs of that high prestige, cleanly abstract, approach.

2.3   Attitudes to speech data

> **Quote 2.1**   Goodwin on attitudes towards speech data in linguistics in the early 1980s
>
> Methodologically, most contemporary linguists do not use actual speech as a source of data for the analysis of linguistic structure. They base this position in part on the argument that the phrasal breaks, such as restarts, found in actual speech give evidence of such defective performance that the data are useless for the study of competence.
>
> (Goodwin, 1981: 12)

From its beginnings as a separately constituted discipline late in the nineteenth century and through the twentieth, linguistics, 'linguistic science' or the 'science of language' has been a little sensitive about being

Quote 2.2 Noam Chomsky on the status and usefulness of natural speech in linguistic analysis

A record of natural speech will show numerous false starts, deviations from rules, changes of plan in mid-course, and so on. The problem for the linguist, as well as for the child learning the language, is to determine from the data of performance the underlying system of rules that has been mastered by the speaker–hearer and that he puts to use in actual performance.

(Chomsky, 1965: 5)

taken seriously as an academic discipline. Early European work on grammar and comparative philology focused largely on uncovering 'laws' and principles governing language change (mainly at the level of individual words) or sought to put the study of the sounds of language on an accurate, systematic and near-scientific footing. The point to note is that, while such approaches used real words or sounds in their investigations, the impetus for the research was to abstract away from these particular instances towards a regular system governed by precisely defined rules.

However, even theoretically oriented work engages with data at some level. At its most basic the research is grounded in some real-world concepts, if not 'hard' data. When researchers think of empirical approaches in opposition to more theoretically oriented ones, it is a matter of what role the data are seen to have in the research process. In 'classical' theoretically oriented, scientific methods, the model or theory on which a study is based is not going to be fundamentally redefined by the outcomes of the research. Data which challenge the prevailing theory are likely to be set aside as 'blips' and more generally the phenomena being investigated will be selected in such a way that they will tend to fit in with the existing paradigm.

This is a pressing issue for the researcher into speech. Recent research into the grammar of spoken discourse has suggested that there are a number of constructions regularly used by speakers (for example, subject–verb ellipsis – 'Nice day' as opposed to 'It is a nice day') which do not fit into the norms of traditional grammar models, or items which have a high occurrence (for example, semi-modal verbs such as 'tend to') but which are presented as 'unusual'.

There are two main reasons why this is the case. The first is to do with the role of theory or the pre-existing model used in planning the research enterprise. New work is founded on previous work, and, in general, researchers find it easier to work with a stable and widely accepted model.

Concept 2.1   **The grammar of speech**

One of the major research questions which remains unanswered is whether there is such a thing as a 'grammar of speech'. This is difficult to decide because people mean different things when they talk about 'grammar' (and, indeed, 'speech'). On the one hand, grammatical items which are frequent in the spoken language can be seen as candidates for inclusion at the core of a spoken grammar. On the other hand, decisions about what is/is not acceptable as part of a pedagogic grammar have never been made statistically in the past. Therefore, before a model of spoken grammar built on frequencies can be adopted by the teaching profession the criteria for the grammar need to be decided. More fundamentally, those who see grammar not as the product of a description but a set of rules will question whether the discourse of individual language users provide sound evidence for these rules.

Traditional grammar, while most people would accept its shortcomings, provides a fairly consistent set of constructs, definitions and structural relations for the new research to be based on. Since a grammatical construct like the relative clause or the noun phrase is relatively stable and clearly defined a researcher will find several hundred articles on the topics with ease. There are two main problems with structures outside the standard definitions. First, by their nature they do not fall into the neat categories of the existing grammar model. Second, there will be no accepted terminology for the elements being described. Thus, a construction typical of spoken English such as the following, 'where he went wrong my mate Tony was not getting the car taxed before he went on his holiday', might be defined as a 'cleft' sentence, 'pre-posed', containing a 'left-shifted head' or other terms which may or may not mean exactly the same thing to everyone or overlap with one another exactly.

The second major reason why there has been little detailed description of the grammar of speech is technological. Initially in the first part of the twentieth century, speech itself was difficult to capture, and even the advent of the tape recorder meant that gathering large samples of data and analysing them were a laborious process. The ability to record speech, and the comparatively recent growth in the power of the personal computer, has brought the possibility of large corpus studies to the office of the applied linguistics lecturer. However, the corpus and corpus analysis tools have tended to lend themselves most readily to lexical research rather than grammatical. In addition, the complexities of capturing large quantities of spontaneous spoken data have meant that most corpora depend for their data on the written mode. Insights from corpora which combine a balance of both spoken and written material are beginning to filter into the public domain in forms which can be used by the teaching community, however.

For instance the *Longman Grammar of Spoken and Written English* or Carter and McCarthy's *Cambridge Advanced Grammar of English*.

Quote 2.3 The *Longman Grammar of Spoken and Written English* on surprises from corpus-based approaches to grammar

[E]ven basic word classes – such as nouns, adjectives, verb, and adverbs – are far from evenly distributed across registers. Nouns and prepositional phrases are much more common in news than in conversation, whereas verbs and adverbs are much more common in conversation. These distributional patterns reflect differing functional priorities. For example, news texts have an informational focus, frequently using nouns to refer to people and things in the world.... In contrast, the interpersonal focus of conversation results in frequent use of verbs to narrate events and to present personal attitudes, while the online production and context dependent circumstances of conversation make it more appropriate to use pronouns instead of nouns.

(Biber *et al.*, 1999: 11)

Concerns about the status of data, the role of the researcher and the benefits of experimental versus naturalistic approaches stay with us today, and the debate in linguistics continues about the status and value of data-focused approaches and particularly the related issue of qualitative versus quantitative research methods. When it comes to the data/theory binary in researching speech the issue is extremely complex.

Concept 2.2   **What unified theories of speech exist?**

Considering the universality of the ability to speak across humankind there has been little attempt to draw together a unified theory of the process. Notable exceptions such as Levelt's seminal work *Speaking: from intention to articulation* (Levelt, 1989) fall outside what is considered core work in applied linguistics, coming under the umbrella of psycholinguistics. Even here work stops largely at the point of utterance and does not pursue the important issues of interaction, the influence of intonation and prosody, turn-taking and so on; nor how these features might relate to one another in a process of communication that is unique to spoken mode.

The kind of research which follows classical scientific paradigms has been criticised within applied linguistics in recent years, particularly in the realm of work carried out by teachers into issues which affect them most directly (broadly called 'Action Research').

Quote 2.4 DePoy and Gitlin on participatory action research

Endogenous research has also been referred to as 'action research' and more recently 'participatory action research' (PAR). This latter term has emerged from research on organizations. Its purpose is to close the gap between multiple interest groups concerned with the study problem. The PAR approach... involves an ongoing exchange between researcher and study participants in the diagnosis and evaluation of problems and in the data gathering process and assessment of findings.

(DePoy and Gitlin, 1993: 136)

Quote 2.5 Nunan on action research for teachers

Is this activity research? I would argue that it is, in that it fits my minimalist definition, containing a question/issue, data, and interpretative analysis. Others may argue that such activity can only lay claims to being research if the teacher has taken steps to guard against threats to the reliability and validity of the research. I believe that care needs to be taken over the reliability of all forms of inquiry, but that for action research there is not the same imperative to deal with external validity. In many cases practitioners are less concerned with generating generalisable knowledge than with solving pressing problems associated with their own particular workplace.

(Nunan, 1992: 18–19)

Quote 2.6 Lazaraton on experimental versus ethnographic methods in SLA research

Clearly, no research approach is suitable for every situation or question. Nevertheless, we might ask why qualitative research is not more prevalent than it is in applied linguistics, given our interest in the social and/or socio-cultural context of language learning and use. Watson-Gegeo (1988) suggests that one reason ethnography is not more widely used in SLA studies is that it views language learning from a language socializations rather than language acquisition perspective, crediting context and culture for much of what happens in the learning environment. Because many of the studies that use elicited, experimental data rarely consider these factors, it is understandable why the approach has not been more widely adopted.

(Lazaraton, 1995: 466)

In this context the concept of the investigator as an objective entity outside the data being analysed and distanced from it is seen as unviable by some. Nevertheless, despite the growing interest in discourse-oriented, socially informed and situated data, the bulk of published research in the field of applied linguistics does not embrace the most contextually sensitive kind of approach: qualitative work. And yet, given the situatedness and context sensitivity of speech data, the qualitative paradigm could be a highly suitable one for the topic.

Quote 2.7 DePoy and Gitlin on naturalistic enquiry

We have said that the overall aim of analysis is to search for patterns, be they descriptive or analytic, simple or complex, that emerge from the information obtained. Some researchers seek to generate theory, whereas others aim to reveal, interpret, and communicate the multiple layers of understandings of human experience that emerge in the field. In naturalistic research, data analysis is based on an inductive thinking process that is ongoing and interspersed with the activity of gathering information.

(de Poy and Gitlin, 1993: 279)

2.4   The applicability of research approaches and frameworks to the study of speech

Robert de Beaugrande (1994) in his paper 'Speech and writing in theory and in data' argues for the need to look at speech data firmly in their own right. His is one of the most sustained and vigorous assertions that linguists prefer to use models of language derived from writing because this helps them in the process of tidying up the data and making it more manageable. In this process and through the representation of speech data in the written form, valuable aspects of the data are lost, de Beaugrande suggests. Using a functionalist framework, he analyses sections of speech data and written samples on equal terms.

The following sections outline some of the major approaches taken to the study of language and discuss their strengths and weaknesses in relation to the study of speech and teaching speaking skills, taking into account how far mode is seen as relevant. Table 2.1 gives an indication of how far, in general, some central approaches in linguistics deal with situated data, and whether they allow the researcher room to deal with speech on its own terms as de Beugrande suggests. In places there are query marks

Table 2.1

	Situated data?	Mode relevant?
Discourse and conversational analysis	✓✓	✓✓
Functional or systemic linguistics	✓✓	✓✓?
Critical linguistics	✓✓	✓?
Corpus linguistics	✓	✓
Socio-linguistics	✓✓	✓?
Phonetics	–	✓✓
Phonology	✓?	✓✓
Psycholinguistics	✓?	✓?
Neurolinguistics	✓?	✓
Second language acquisition	✓?	–
Computational linguistics	–	–
Morphology	–	–
Semantics	–	–
Syntax	–	–
Transformational grammar	–	–

where the general approach or epistemology of the discipline would permit this aspect, but for whatever reason it is not apparent in work in the field. For example, although functional or systemic linguistics is strongly in favour of acknowledging the influence of mode on discourse there has been, with the notable exception of Halliday (1989), little attention to speech as a separate entity to be studied in its own right. Equally in the case of critical linguistics a great deal of attention has been paid to the role of literacy and, by definition therefore, written forms in isolation from others, but little work on to what extent people may be empowered by explicit focus on the skill of speaking.

Socio-linguistic work, for example, on the social marking carried by a particular phoneme or the speaking strategies of a particular racial group, shows that the discipline draws its data from the spoken mode but again does not relate findings to any broader theory of speech.

It is notable that the most strongly influential theoretical branches of linguistics – morphology, syntax, semantics, transformational grammar – and the applied disciplines which relate closely to them – computational linguistics and second language acquisition – not only do not place high value on situated data (with notable exceptions such as Katherina Bremer *et al.*'s 1996 SLA-oriented study of immigrant workers' interactions within their receiving society) but also regard mode as largely irrelevant.

Hand in hand with a removal of the object of study to the theoretical, unsituated, or abstract level is a convenient merging of the construct 'speech' with 'language'. It is convenient because it permits the models in question to use isolated examples closer to the norms of formal, published written mode and ignore deviant, ill-formed and difficult to parse forms which might come under debate if real-world examples of speech (and, indeed, writing) were the basis for the model. Secondly, such abstract approaches permit the theorist to ignore sound-based meaning bearing elements of language, such as intonation, which are again less easy to formalise than text-based elements.

Much of a person's identity and communicative force is carried by the vocal pattern which we associate with them, and many of the affective aspects of language reach the world via the slightest changes in voice quality. In teaching spoken language one might imagine these aspects would be seen as of highest importance. However, since most abstract language paradigms do not take into account or try to account for aspects of the dynamic, interpersonally oriented mode that is speech, the focus tends to fall on structural input, disengaged both from its discourse context and its meaning-bearing 'music'.

From the above I hope it is becoming clear that there are complex reasons for there not being a unified theory of speech in linguistics or applied linguistics. Not least, I have been arguing that it is a problem that several of the most central paradigms in linguistic science regard mode as irrelevant.

2.5   The problem of the status of speech in applied linguistics

As mentioned in Chapter 1, the spoken form is, in one sense, very highly valued in linguistics and applied linguistics. It is the primary form of a language and the source of innovation and language change. In the realm of second language teaching there is also apparently high attention paid to the skill of speaking: to be fluent in a language is the lay person's goal; the source of input in highly influential 'communicative approaches' is largely the spoken form, and as have previously noted in general there has tended to be a conflation in linguistics of the term 'language' with 'speech' as if the two are interchangeable and learning to speak is what is involved in learning a new language.

This is perhaps due to the dominance of the child language acquisition paradigm which influenced theories of second language acquisition throughout the twentieth century. Thus the primacy of the spoken form in first language acquisition (since no child learns to write before they learn to speak, the spoken mode is the only mode available for consideration and therefore the issue of distinguishing 'language' from 'speech' is irrelevant) is mapped on to theories of second language acquisition. However, paradoxically, there is very little attention paid to the spoken form in its own right in the world of linguistics, or of language teaching. For example, a survey of key journals in the field will find many more articles dealing explicitly with the written form than with the spoken. There is a similar 'invisibility' factor at work in the teaching and researching of the skill of listening (see also Rost, 2002) in this series for further discussion of listening as a discrete skill).

2.6   Where are the data for research into speech?

One of the difficulties in researching speech is the fact that, unlike written texts, the notion of a free-standing genre or clearly delimited sample to be investigated does not readily lend itself to speech. Whereas the researcher into writing can, if they wish, start from a relatively well-defined set of texts which clearly fit into a category (newspaper language, popular fiction, advertising texts, academic writing and so on) the researcher into speech will generally find no such helpful categories to hand. Writing presents itself in front of the researcher through the materiality of its visual medium. The researcher into speech must usually look beyond the discourse to the context in order to delimit the data under investigation and to ensure they are comparing like with like.

2.6.1   Analysing speaking skills at the level of discourse

When we consider the level of discourse we are thinking about how speakers interact with one another (for example, how they know when it is their turn to speak) and how talk is organised in particular kinds of patterns over long stretches of language (for example, how speakers structure their talk for listeners so that they can follow changes in topic easily).

During the 1970s and 1980s the main concern in the field was to consider where the discourse level of language fitted in with current views of language, and to what extent regularities or even 'rules' of interaction could be uncovered. This focus on rule-based paradigms reflected the dominant model for language which had grown up in the USA. Seminal work was carried out in America by conversational analysts who developed highly sophisticated systems for representing language features which had previously been studied very little for example laughter or pauses or apparently trivial utterances, such as 'uh huh' or 'oh' (e.g. Schegloff, 1981). This detailed investigation into the mechanics of conversation led to concepts such as 'openings', 'closings', 'pair parts', 'formulaic exchanges' or the 'turn relevance point' (TRP).

Concept 2.3   **Turn relevance point (TRP)**

This is a moment in speaking when several linguistic features combine to signal to an interlocutor that they could take over the speaker role. In Anglophone cultures these tend to be the ends of clauses and are signalled by pitch, intonation, pace, micro-pausing as well as extra-linguistic features such as gaze. Next time you are in a free-flowing conversation you might like to stand back (or better still record a conversation) and see how speakers know that they can begin to speak without seeming to interrupt one another. For many learners of a language, ability to speak is not the factor which isolates them in a conversation. Rather it is the inability to 'read' the moments when they might be able to begin to speak.

In the UK key features of the structuring of discourse were investigated and notions such as 'discourse markers', 'transactions' and 'exchanges' were developed.

Concept 2.4   **Discourse markers**

These are words 'outside' clauses which carry little or no meaning in their own right but signal something to the listener about the structure or organisation of the talk, for example 'right' or 'ok' in English. As well as logical relations, discourse markers can signal more subtle aspects of talk: 'well' can indicate reservation or hesitation; 'now' can indicate a change in topic; 'actually' can mean many things including difference of opinion or correction or even defensiveness (cf. English cooking is very good. English cooking is very good, actually.). Because learners are usually taught a form of the language which is strongly influenced by written mode, spoken discourse markers are not given high prominence in a syllabus, if they are taught explicitly at all. This can leave a learner floundering both in terms of listening to conversation and taking part. Discourse markers oil the wheels of talk, and conversation without them can seem very 'cranky'.

Both discourse analysis and conversation analysis have links to socio-linguistics in that they prefer not to deal with samples of language in isolation and conversation analysis in particular is interested in the relations between interlocutors. Discourse analysis, however, has traditionally tended to concentrate on longer sections of language and focussed on interrelations between different sections of text. Within this the discourse analyst is interested in how speakers carry out functions of language and the choices made by them in different contexts.

In terms of the application of some of the main ideas of conversation and discourse analysis, but with a stronger focus on the former, Brown and Yule (1983) *Teaching the Spoken Language: An approach based on the analysis of conversational English* provide something of a bridge between the schools of thought outlined above and more practically classroom-oriented applications. Interestingly, despite the crucial aspects of speech which discourse-level studies have uncovered they have, on the whole, been very slow to trickle down into classroom teaching and published teaching materials in general. There have been books for teachers on the topic (for example, McCarthy, 1991, *Discourse Analysis for Language Teachers* or Evelyn Hatch's, 1992, very different *Discourse and Language Education*). Carter, Hughes and McCarthy (2000) attempts to bring some of the complexities of spoken grammar in discourse to the classroom via grammar materials.

Discourse analysis in the UK does, however, have strong incidental links to the classroom in that much of the most influential early work (for example, Sinclair and Coulthard, 1975) was carried out on classroom interaction. These classic studies, which generated some of the fundamental categories of discourse analysis, were based on teacher–pupil talk.

The relationship between psychology and speech behaviour is another thread to research into global aspects of speech, and one which again links in with the bigger questions of how spoken language data relate to underlying linguistic systems, whether neurological, biological or genetic. Whereas discourse or conversation analysts will describe patterns of speech behaviour in order to uncover regularities in the organisation of spoken discourse, and will see these patterns of interest in themselves, the psychologist will generally regard utterances as a source of evidence of mental or behavioural processes. So, for example, whereas a discourse or conversation analyst may look at a feature such as patterns of repetition in speech and see how far they can generalise about lexical repetition in its own right, the psychologist would investigate how such repetitions relate to how humans process complex utterances, or the timing and levels of pre-planning.

Research summary   Speech errors and psychological processes

Clark and Wasow (1998) investigated a typical pattern of repetition either PRONOUN + PAUSE/FILLER + PRONOUN (I uh I (think)...) or ARTICLE + PAUSE/FILLER + ARTICLE (The uh the (problem)...) and suggested that the different stages in this pattern related to the way in which speakers committed themselves to an utterance and that these items were an integral part of the underlying psychological processes by which utterances reach the world.

In terms of teaching languages, the fields of higher-level studies into speech described here open up several questions and ways forward, particularly in relation to uncovering differences between cultures in terms of how conversation is organised. This in turn can help learners and teachers understand potential pitfalls in language interaction which are not due to any grammatical mistake but different pragmatic and cultural expectations.

2.6.2   The research space at the level of language choices: grammar and vocabulary

Research into speech at the level of grammar and vocabulary in its own right is relatively hard to find. David Brazil's (1995) *A Grammar of Speech* is unusual because the linear nature of speech production is taken seriously and talk is described in terms of having 'purpose'. It is interesting to note that, although Brazil's book is highly regarded, the teaching profession as a whole has found it difficult to assimilate many of the principles which underpin the work. The class text on pronunciation for advanced learners of English also by David Brazil (Brazil, 1994) presents a similar unification of discourse level and other meaning-bearing language features. Hence, in many ways Brazil's work represents one of the most consistent attempts to look at the spoken form on its own terms.

Klein and Purdue (1992) *Utterance Structure: Developing grammars again* is another notable exception to the rule. In this the authors take issue with many of the assumptions of second language acquisition and base their analysis on the notion that learner utterances are a language to be studied in their own right (rather than in relation to a 'target' language). The book is of particular interest to the researcher into speech because it takes a strongly empirical (data oriented) stand and builds the discussion on real utterances. However, the researcher new to speech research studies, reading either of these books, should realise that while both of them are fascinating neither of them have succeeded in becoming centrally accepted into the inner circle of applied linguistics, partly due to their (deliberate) lack of overlap with the theories underlying the field more generally.

Starting points for research into speaker choices at this level might be more usefully found embedded in studies on register variation, or differences between speech and writing. This is because there has been more work done on these aspects, and more work that has gained currency over the years. A particular area within the field to look for inspiration for research topics is corpus linguistics. Douglas Biber's work, and most notably his influential *Variation Across Speech and Writing* (Biber, 1988), gives a strongly data-oriented analysis of a wide variety of spoken and written sources, concluding that certain grammatical features cluster together to make up the distinctive style of a spoken or written genre. These features in turn map on to dimensions of contrast, such as whether the language is concerned with conveying information or is more interpersonally oriented. Rather than suggesting a simple binary division between speech and writing Biber suggests that there are patterns of probability among language features which show statistical regularity in how they co-occur in spoken and written genres.

Corpus-based work can also help inform research into speech on aspects such as tenses (Aarts and Meyer, 1995) vocabulary (Stenström, 1990), clauses (Nelson, 1997), ellipsis (Meyer, 1995). Academics have also been working on bridging the gap between corpus findings and the classroom (e.g. Johns, 1991; Tribble and Jones, 1990; Knowles, 1990; and most relevantly for the spoken mode, Svartvik, 1991), but since the availability of spoken corpora is a relatively recent phenomenon, the focus of much work had tended to be on written texts.

Gaining access to spoken corpora is becoming gradually easier and for the researcher or teacher who wants to begin their own project a number of avenues are now open. These range from sampling a larger corpus on-line (for example, you can try out the British National Corpus at: http://sara.natcorp.ox.ac.uk/lookup.html) to ordering a corpus or a sample on a CD-ROM (for example via ICAME at http://www.hd.uib.no/icame/newcd.htm) to gaining full access for scholarly work either via the corpus designers or publishers associated with the project. For further details, see Chapter 10.

However, the use of real speech data in research is not without problems. One of the great advantages of an a-modal view of language is that it side-steps several fundamental questions which arise when contextualised language between actual people is analysed.

Not only are there grammatical, lexical and structural variations within a spoken language in a country, say between geographical areas or social classes, there are perhaps more significant differences in the case of English between the varieties now spoken in different parts of the world. As English becomes ever increasingly the common language of the world it is clear that the tiny number of speakers of 'standard' English based in Britain is far outnumbered by the speakers of other varieties of English: fluent, easily understood, but different in grammar and vocabulary from the root source. As soon as one turns from abstract models of grammar and syntax towards models which might reflect the patterns found in real speech, the interesting issue arises of 'which grammar' one is actually describing. This question is rather more pressing for the language teacher than for the descriptive linguist.

2.6.3   The research space at the level of speech production: fluency and pronunciation

Traditionally a great deal of research into phonology is undertaken to find evidence of an underlying system, particularly in relation to the dominant model of language in the mid to late twentieth century in the transformational or the universal grammar paradigm. Within this paradigm some consideration is given to the interplay between the different levels, and the direction of influence. However, the aim of the work is to find evidence of internal language knowledge rather than to describe the system for any applied purpose. For example, Berg and Hassan (1996) examined speaker errors in three languages but were less interested in classifying or explaining the errors than in gaining insight into the 'mapping' or hierarchical conceptualisation of speakers' linguistic knowledge in the three cases.

In contrast to this approach, work into pedagogically related phonology exists within a much less theoretically oriented, and generally experimentally based framework. Experimental style research into the teaching of pronunciation is an area which can provide clearly relevant results for the classroom. For instance, the type of classroom-oriented experiment which has been carried out in this way can be found in Derwing Monro and Wiebe (1998). These researchers compared pronunciation instruction methods across three groups of learners over a 12 week course. One group had no instruction (acting as a control group), a second was instructed at the level of individual sound features and the third was taught about higher-level factors, such as intonation. At the level of random sentences, both the groups who were taught pronunciation made progress. However, the levels of comprehensibility of the group given instruction into global, prosodic features in terms of narrative production were higher.

Keeping up to date with these kinds of results can help teachers plan the balance of the speaking syllabus, and can also account for contrasts between student progress in and outside the classroom, for example, if a student appears to be making good progress in pronunciation in controlled circumstances but remains difficult to understand when producing longer sections of speech.

2.7 Summary

This chapter reviewed some classical approaches to the research process and addressed the particular problems for the researcher working with spoken forms of language. Beside the issue of the lack of extensive work on the spoken form in its own right, I raised the question of the role of speech data in language theory generally, and of the attitude to situated spoken discourse as the basis for generalisations about language. In relation to research based around teaching the spoken form, the further issue of the cultural and pragmatic problems raised by real speech data was aired.

Further reading

One of the most innovative approaches to the analysis of language in terms of the stream of speech can be found in:

Brazil, D. (1995). *A Grammar of Speech*. Oxford: Oxford University Press.

A range of spoken samples with accompanying cassette and extensive line by line commentary can be found in:

Carter, R. and McCarthy, M. (1997). *Exploring Spoken English*. Cambridge, Cambridge University Press.

A brief but seminal text remains:

Halliday, M. A. K. (1989). *Spoken and Written Language*. Oxford: Oxford University Press.

An up-to-date overview of qualitiative methods and the issue of what counts as data for research can be found in:

Holliday, A. (2001). *Doing and Writing Qualitative Research*. Thousand Oaks, CA: Sage Publications.

A clear introduction to the importance of speech data for the language classroom is:

McCarthy, M. (1991). *Discourse Analysis for Language Teachers*. Cambridge: Cambridge University Press.

An approach which places high value on intonation and context can be found in:

Pennington, M. C. (1996). *Phonology in Language Teaching*. London: Longman.

II Issues for teaching and assessing speaking

Approaches, materials and the problem of 'real' speech

This chapter will ...

- look at the skill of speaking from three different perspectives: global interactive skills, structural choices and patterns found in speech, issues of pronunciation and fluency;

- describe some of the approaches and materials used to teach speaking skills;

- discuss the question of how far speaking can be taught in ways which make it divorced from culture and context.

3.1 Introduction

What is the overriding objective of a speaking component in a language teaching syllabus? It seems a tautology to suggest that it is to enable the student to speak the target language. However, it is in teasing out the notion of what the 'target' actually is that the complexity of this question becomes evident.

As teachers, and indeed researchers, we have preconceptions about the spoken form which influence our beliefs about it. These, often strongly literacy influenced views, affect how we think about speech at the level of interaction, at the level of language choices and in what we think it means to be a 'fluent' speaker. A similar issue arises in many of the resource books and materials for teachers on the spoken mode.

To support the communicative 'revolution' in teaching methods, there has been a raft of published materials and text books for the teacher.

Although now a little dated, Byrne (1986) remains a classic handbook for language teachers on oral skills. The reason that this book has been reprinted and re-edited so many times since its first publication in 1976 is that, although it does not deal explicitly with communicative approaches as they are defined in the broader and more up-to-date theories of language learning, it does address the key underlying assumption of much of the communicative approach, viz that teachers and learners must accommodate 'language learning to the unfavourable environment of the classroom' (Byrne, 1986: 1).

Other publications also focus on the issue of the difficulties of reproducing realistic communicative contexts for language learning students. The sections on oral work in Cross (1992) *Practical Handbook of Language Teaching*, particularly those on elicitation techniques and exploiting dialogues, provide a thoughtful starting point for the student teacher. Cross is insightful enough to explore some of the issues around the nature of speech, the problem of inauthenticity of classroom discourse and so on, and yet provides a very practical hands-on approach to the subject.

Bygate (1987) provides a task-based approach to understanding some of the basic issues of handling spoken interaction. Beginning from the notion that oral communication needs to be conceptualised as a skill rather than as knowledge, the author outlines the distinctive nature of speech (for example, its reciprocal nature), differences between speech and writing (particularly in terms of 'processing conditions'), interaction skills (particularly the negotiation of meaning and the management of discourse), and first versus second language communication strategies. This book also provides good guidelines on how to categorise and choose speaking tasks, and is a very readable 'bridge' between more academic publications and the classroom.

Penny Ur's chapter on teaching speaking in Ur (1996) is an excellent, teacher-friendly introduction to the main techniques for dealing with speaking tasks, covering fluency practice, topic vs. task-focused speaking activities, discussion activities, other interactions, role play and oral testing. Nolasco and Arthur (1987) is even more practically oriented giving over 100 classroom activities on speaking and conversation. This is one of the few books to draw out distinctions between not only fluency/accuracy, fluency/appropriacy but also some differences between speaking skills and conversational skills.

Wingate (1993) deals with the problem of fostering speech in the classroom with low-level learners and provides a useful overview of the main principles and techniques for eliciting speech as well as a range of around 40 potential classroom activities.

On the less practical side, Brown and Yule (1983) attempt to link discussion of the particular problems of dealing with speech in teaching contexts, for example the issue of how to grade speaking tasks. The most successful chapter in this is the discussion and summary of testing oral skills. Also existing on the interface between academic and pedagogic are *Language as Discourse* (McCarthy and Carter, 1994) and *Discourse Analysis for Language Teachers* (McCarthy, 1991).

However, what should be noted is that in the majority of these texts and approaches little explicit attention (comparable to that given to the written mode) is paid to the nature of the speech itself in terms of style, register, levels of formality and so on; particularly in terms of linking grammatical/ structural choices and discourse context. This leads to a paradoxical situation. The spoken mode is strongly upheld as the primary source of language acquisition and is fostered and facilitated as a central activity in the language classroom, but this is linked to an underlying language acquisition objective, rather than to helping learners understand the peculiarities of speech, and the sensitivity of language choices made by speakers to individual, cultural and discourse factors.

3.2 Spoken interaction in context

Much research into the global aspects of speech production has traditionally been subsumed under sister disciplines of applied linguistics, such as pragmatics, socio-linguistics or ethno-linguistics. These three associated disciplines share a common interest in the relationship between language and social interaction. The most linguistically oriented discipline is pragmatics.

Concept 3.1   **Pragmatics**

This field is interested in the language 'rules' which govern, say, politeness conventions in a particular culture. Within pragmatics there are different approaches to research questions. Formal pragmatics is most interested in rules and rule-like patterns in discourse. In this area a researcher might be most concerned with the constraints on the use of particular expressions in conversation (see, for example, Gundel, Hedberg and Zacharski, 1993). Inter-language pragmatics, on the other hand, as the term suggests, is focused on the issues surrounding differences in conversational behaviour between cultures (see Rose and Kasper, 2001).

However, at the level of global interactive skills, whether in the field of pragmatics or, more broadly, socio-linguistics or ethnography, it is rare to find researchers investigating spoken data to discover something about the faculty of speech itself. While all three disciplines will in their different ways use samples of speech to carry out their research, the objective will be to reach conclusions about matters beyond the spoken form. For example, in cross-cultural pragmatics researchers may look at the use of thanking expressions and responses and the differences between two societies in this area; but, although the medium of speech is the source of data, the focus is not on the investigation of a sub-genre of the spoken form but rather on the issue of cultural difference.

3.3 Teaching global speaking skills

There is a good range of published materials which, without drawing directly on the insights of academic work such as that outlined above, can be categorised as dealing with the skill of speaking, and dealing with it at the level of speaker interactions in context, which is the focus of this first section of this chapter.

I will be describing a number of resource books and classroom materials on the topic of speaking. In addition, I will use some of these to exemplify the tendency to divorce speech data from realistic social contexts and the implications of this for teaching the spoken form of a language. Throughout I will be using English language as the case study, but the points made are intended to be generalisable to other language contexts.

A good starting point for those who are unfamiliar with some of the ideas behind conversation or discourse analysis is Nolasco and Arthur (1987). This is a resource book for teachers on the topic of conversation. The introduction provides an overview of some of the main features which applied linguists study: turn taking, adjacency pairs, conversational appropriacy, gender differences and so on. There is a section on giving feedback to students on their conversational performance and some of the techniques described could be adapted to provide data for action research projects.

One of the most challenging tasks can be teaching interactive skills to lower levels of students. Marion Geddes and Gill Sturtridge's (1992) *Elementary Conversation* as its title suggests helps lower-level students focus on conversational skills from a very early stage, including elements such as how to open and close a conversation (see Quote 3.1), or how to show interest. The units contain summaries of structural forms to aid the learner. Such lists of phrases and sentences remain a common feature of materials on speaking which provide the learner with a sense of security and of progression.

A popular text at higher levels which also provides structural items as prompts on each page is Keller and Warner's (1988) *Conversation Gambits* (see Quote 3.2).

Everyday Listening and Speaking by Sarah Cunningham and Peter Moor (1992) is less conversationally oriented but combines some useful language work in a variety of contexts at the intermediate level. The book contrasts with the two previous examples in that it integrates structural items being presented into the tasks themselves (see Quote 3.3).

| Quote 3.1 | Phrase box |

Initial greetings	How are you?	Fine thanks. And you?
	How are things?	Great.
	How are you doing?	Pretty good.
	Everything OK?	OK.
	How's life?	Alright.
	How's it going?	Not bad. Not too bad.
		So so.

Follow-up questions	How's your mother?	She's very well, thanks.

Please give her my best wishes.

I haven't seen you for ages.

Have you been | away?
             | sick?
             | ill?
             | off work?

Everything OK?

(Are you very) busy?   Quite | busy.
                        Pretty |

(Are you still) enjoying your | job?
                                 | English course?
                                 | holiday?

Moving to someone else	There's (David). I must say hello. I'll speak to you later (Gillian).

Explaining past illness	I had (a touch of) flu.

I had | a cold.
       | a sore throat.
       | a bad cough.
       | a bad back.
       | a stomach upset.

Expressing sympathy	I'm sorry to hear that. Are you OK now? alright

Making sure two people know each other	You've met A. Do you know A? Yes, we've known each other for ages.

(M. Geddes and G. Sturtridge, *Elementary Conversation*, Macmillan Education, 1992)

Quote 3.2 Arguments and Counter-arguments

Very often, when we have a plan, someone has an objection or a reservation. We then have to think up a counter-argument to try to persuade them.

In this dialogue the husband is trying to persuade his wife that they need a cottage in the country.

Him: Why don't we buy a cottage in the country – somewhere we could go at weekends and for holidays. **(Plan)**

Her: That's a good idea, but don't you think the children will get bored – can't you hear them – not the cottage AGAIN this summer! **(Reservation)**

Him: That's probably true, but I think it would be nice for us, and after all, it won't be long before they'll want to go off with their own friends. **(Counter-argument)**

Work in pairs with these ideas using the phrases for reservations and counter-arguments.

1. A: take up skiing
   B: don't have the time or money
   A: it would be fun, good exercise

2. A: buy a flat
   B: can't afford it
   A: cheaper than paying rent

3. A: fly to Moscow
   B: cheaper to go by train
   A: we'd lose a week of holiday just travelling, plus all the money on food

4. A: buy a new car – the old one's rusty
   B: we haven't finished paying for the old one
   A: the old one's dangerous

5. A: have a party
   B: the neighbours would object
   A: why not invite the neighbours

6. A: your plan
   B: your reservation
   A: your counter-argument

Reservation

Yes, but ...

Yes, but don't forget ...

That would be great, except ...

That's a good idea, but ...

Counter-arguments

Even so,

Even if that is so,

That may be so, but ...

That's probably true, but ...

Possibly, but ...

(E. Keller and S. T. Warner, *Conversation Gambits* (*Real English Conversation Practices*), Language Teaching Publications, 1988)

Quote 3.3 Everyday listening and speaking

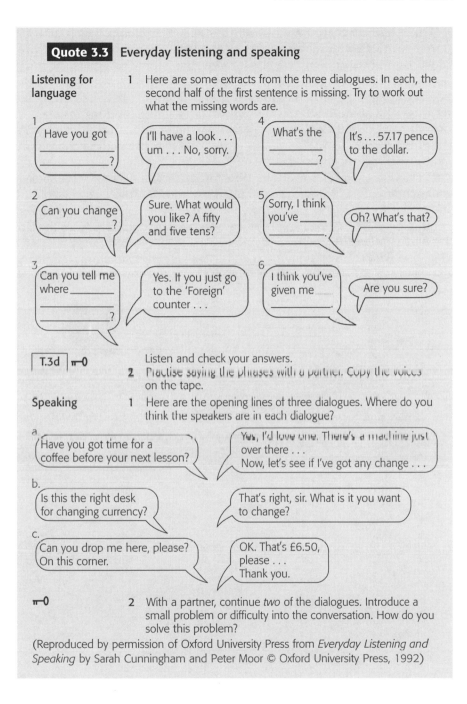

Listening for language

1 Here are some extracts from the three dialogues. In each, the second half of the first sentence is missing. Try to work out what the missing words are.

1
Have you got
_____
_____?

I'll have a look . . .
um . . . No, sorry.

4
What's the
_____
_____?

It's . . . 57.17 pence
to the dollar.

2
Can you change
_____?

Sure. What would
you like? A fifty
and five tens?

5
Sorry, I think
you've _____
_____.

Oh? What's that?

3
Can you tell me
where_____
_____
_____?

Yes. If you just go
to the 'Foreign'
counter . . .

6
I think you've
given me _____
_____.

Are you sure?

T.3d ☛

Listen and check your answers.

2 Practise saying the phrases with a partner. Copy the voices on the tape.

Speaking

1 Here are the opening lines of three dialogues. Where do you think the speakers are in each dialogue?

a
Have you got time for a
coffee before your next lesson?

Yes, I'd love one. There's a machine just
over there . . .
Now, let's see if I've got any change . . .

b.
Is this the right desk
for changing currency?

That's right, sir. What is it you want
to change?

c.
Can you drop me here, please?
On this corner.

OK. That's £6.50,
please . . .
Thank you.

☛

2 With a partner, continue *two* of the dialogues. Introduce a small problem or difficulty into the conversation. How do you solve this problem?

(Reproduced by permission of Oxford University Press from *Everyday Listening and Speaking* by Sarah Cunningham and Peter Moor © Oxford University Press, 1992)

Three questions are raised by all these kinds of books which, in their different ways and at different levels, provide structural cues at the level of words, phrase or complete clause. The first is how complete the items listed are. In several cases, in my experience, teachers' own copies of the books contain scribbled additions to lists which have arisen in their own lessons. The second is the issue of how far speaker level (as opposed to overall 'Language Level') is represented by the grammatical items chosen. And finally little if any attention is given to how far structural choices are genre, speaker or context specific.

Perhaps the most central question for materials dealing with spoken interaction is that of appropriacy in context and the role of social context in language choices. A fascinating, but not always successful, attempt at combining conversational appropriacy and language practice from the late 1970s is *Making Polite Noises* by Roger Hargreaves and Mark Fletcher (1979) in which a selection of structures for language functions are introduced which the student is then required to insert into a taped dialogue (see Quote 3.4).

Quote 3.4   Starting and finishing conversations and showing interest

Sorry to interrupt but	is that a . . . . . ?
Excuse me,	didn't we meet in . . . . . ?
	aren't you . . . . . ?
	I hear you're a . . . . .

Really? Do they? Is she? Mmmm . . . . .
How are you getting on with the . . . . . ?
What was the . . . . . like?
What did you think of the . . . . . ?
How interesting, but how . . . . . ?
Tell me about the . . . . .

Will you excuse me, I'm
afraid I must go and see if . . . . .
say hello to . . . . .
get on with . . . . .

It's been very interesting talking to you.
I've enjoyed hearing about . . . . .
I'd better go and . . . . .
See you again soon, I hope.

Dialogue 1
A: Fascinating. I didn't know it could be done like that.
B: Oh yes. And I've got more photos upstairs . . .

A: Really? But I'm afraid we really must be going now. Thank you for a lovely evening.

B: We've enjoyed it too. We're very glad you could come.

Dialogue 2
A: I've been looking at your brooch. It's very unusual. Where did you get it?

B: I got it in Malaysia.

A: Oh did you? How long were you there? By the way I'm John Gooch...

B: I'm Sylvia Martin. I was out there for three years actually.

A: Really? That must've been a fascinating experience. How did you like the people...?

A few minutes later

A: Good lord! How strange! Well, it's been very interesting talking to you Sylvia. I must go and have a word with some people over by the door, so will you excuse me a moment? See you later I hope.

Scenario
You:

A: Yes, it's American. My uncle gave it to me.

You:

A: He used to but he's retired now.

You:

A: Just for a short time – when I was a student.

You:

A: It was. Everything was so different.

You:

Situations
1. You are sitting in a café. A friend arrives with two companions and introduces you. After a short time you have to leave. What do you say?
2. You are in a colleague's office. He wants to tell you about his weekend but you are in rather a hurry. What do you say?
3. A friend has started to build a garage in his garden. Show interest.
4. A friend tells you he went to Saltwood Castle on Saturday. Show interest.
5. Your friend has been talking about Saltwood Castle for the last twenty minutes. How do you get away?

(M. Hargreaves and M. Fletcher, *Making Polite Noises*, Third Impression, 1989)

One of the problems with this approach is that the notion of what is polite or appropriate is wholly divorced from any social, or indeed any realistic conversational, context.

Many of the pair-work books which grew out of the drive for communicative materials in the classroom during the 1980s and early 1990s also

Quote 3.5 In the pub

1. You are sitting at a table in a pub having a quiet drink on your own. You do not know your partner who is sitting opposite you at the same table. As your partner leaves, your drink, which was half-full, is upset all over everywhere.
    Respond naturally when your partner starts.

2. It is early evening. You have been for a drink with your partner whom you know slightly but not very well. You bought the first round and your partner has bought a round too.
    You are killing time because you are meeting a friend (not your partner) to go to the cinema in half an hour or so, so you would rather like another drink. You think your partner is rather a serious sort of person and are fairly sure that when you offer another drink he will say no. If he does, try to persuade him to have one. Insist if necessary!
    You start.

3. Last night you bought a drink for your partner who popped into the pub while you were having a quiet drink.
    It's now lunch time and a very warm day so you have popped in 'for a quick half'. Your partner is standing at the bar with a drink. Unfortunately, one of the reasons your partner is an acquaintance and not a friend is because you think he is rather mean. You're quite sure you have bought more drinks for him than he has for you.
    You start:
    Oh, hello, did you get there on time last night?

4. You are sitting in a pub talking to some friends. You left your (nearly full) drink on the table behind you.
    Respond naturally when your partner starts.

(M. Lewis, *Partners 3: More Demanding Pair Work Practices*, Language Teaching Publications, 1982)

fall into this trap, even at the higher levels of language competence where contextual, social and discoursal features could be explored in more detail. For example, *Partners 3* by Michael Lewis (1982), while it contains a range of ingenious scenarios and prompts for the more advanced learner (see Quote 3.5), again asks the student to carry out their interactions in something of a void or as if the scenarios being presented were culturally universal or neutral.

Interestingly, in the fields of ESP and EAP the tendency to isolate speaking processes from broader contextual matters has never been as strong as in general language teaching. For example, in Lynch and Anderson's (1992) *Study Speaking* (see Quote 3.6) or Rignall and Furneaux's (1997) *Speaking* in the English for Academic Study Series, speaking skills are embedded in broader functional areas (such as disagreeing) and in turn presented within appropriate real-world contexts and genres (such as the academic seminar). This highlights the advantage of knowing the specific use to which a learner will put a target language in terms of defining the areas to be introduced into a syllabus. While these appropriacy constraints apply across all skill areas, they are more sensitive in the domain of speech.

Two books which can be used to exemplify the strengths and weaknesses of the speech in isolation versus the speech in context approach are Adrian Wallwork's (1997) resource book for speaking activities: *Discussions A–Z* and Carter and McCarthy's (1997) *Exploring Spoken English*. Wallwork's book is an extremely teacher-friendly, photocopiable resource book (see Quote 3.7), with a better than usual range of diverse, engaging and often witty topics and visual stimuli for discussion work. Its aim is to engender discussion and it meets this aim extremely well. These are materials to be handled by a teacher experienced in group work as there is little guidance for the novice, but they will almost inevitably get students talking.

The nature of discussion is dealt with briefly in the introduction but beyond that the material is simply there to function as a prompt rather than to raise awareness about matters such as the nature of interactions during discussion, cultural differences between discussions in different contexts or any socio-linguistic issues underlying debate or argument. In this sense the book is solidly in the tradition of the past thirty years in language teaching, which holds that it is imperative for the student to engage in activities which generate speech and that such activities will in themselves promote language acquisition through processes similar to first language development.

In contrast, a book such as *Exploring Spoken English* focuses on the processes of talk and uses these as starting points for discussion (see Quote 3.8). As a classroom text it will be less easily incorporated into the standard language-learning context, since it requires advanced competence on the part of students and a high degree of confidence in handling language awareness raising tasks on the part of the teacher.

These two books are interesting examples at the two extremes of distinctive perspectives on the role of speech in the classroom context. The former represents a classroom tool which will encourage lively and engaging speaking events to emerge and be sustained. These spoken interactions are in themselves the object of the classroom event. In assessing the success or failure of the section of a lesson based on the material, a significant

Quote 3.6   Seminar skills: questioning

Speakers are expected to allow time at the end of their presentation for questions and discussion. Many people would say that this question-and-answer stage is at least as important as the initial presentation. However, questioning can be a problematic aspect of seminar performance. Often the speaker misunderstands a question (and not only when the questioner is a non-native speaker), because the point is lost in an over-long sentence.

A practical solution is to keep your question short. Don't forget that the presenter may not be sure, when you start to speak, that you are asking a question – you might be wanting to disagree. So you need to make clear:

Example:

a) that it's a question   *'I have a question…*
b) what the topic is   *… about assessment on the course.*
c) what the point is   *What is the overall balance between the examinations and the project work?'*

Discussion point 1
It is sometimes suggested that the speaker should repeat or summarise each question asked from the audience, before beginning to give an answer. Why is this advice given?

Discussion point 2
Questions and answers are not always straightforward. *The speaker* who is asked a question by a listener may understand the question but be unable (or unwilling) to give an answer, in which case, they may *avoid* giving a direct answer. Below are some examples. Can you think of others?

> Avoiding an answer
> *(X) is important but it's too complex for us to deal with here.*
> *I think we have to focus on (Y) rather than (X).*
> *It's too early for us to say whether…*
> *We don't have enough evidence to show that…*
> *That's not something I've had time to deal with, but…*

Discussion point 3
The listener may want to say that the answer they have received is inadequate:

> Following up a question
> *That's not really what I was asking. My question was about…*
> *Perhaps I didn't make my question clear. In fact what I asked was…*
> *I think you've answered a slightly different question.*
> *I've understood that but what I actually had in mind was…*

These expressions are relatively polite and formal. What words could you omit from each example to make them more direct? What type of words are they?

(T. Lynch and K. Anderson, *Study Speaking*, Cambridge University Press, 1992)

Quote 3.7 Are you a good lover?

1   *Love* is an art which needs to be learned if it is to be practised well.
2   You can *love* someone too much.
3   A man and woman can be really good friends without being in *love*.
4   Women have deeper relationships with same-sex friends than men.
5   Men are more attracted to women who are hard to get.
6   Women should never make the first move.
7   You cannot be truly in *love* with two people at the same time.
8   You should only have eyes for your *lover*.
9   It is impossible to *love* and be wise.
10 *Love* can never be forever.

A kiss is just a kiss?

While the language of love making may be universal when two people are from the same culture, the act of kissing can mean very different things in different parts of the world.

In China for example, kissing someone in public is seen as unhygienic and repulsive. In Japan, it may be tolerated, but only if the couple stand with bodies well apart and lips shut tight. And the Inuits of Alaska wouldn't dream of doing anything more oral than rubbing noses – not out of any moral scruples but because Inuit women tend to use their mouths for more everyday tasks such as cleaning oil lamps and chewing animal hides to soften them up.

Even if your intentions aren't amorous, you can still run into trouble. Many a foreigner has come unstuck when greeting a friend who is Dutch (mandatory three cheek-pecks) or French (two only).

1   Men kissing each other is disgusting.
2   Shaking hands is the best way to greet someone.
3   Kissing relatives is always embarrassing.
4   Scenes from films which show lovers kissing should be cut.
5   Couples should not be allowed to kiss in the street, on the bus, at the cinema, at school, at work.

(A. Wallwork, *Discussions A–Z Intermediate*, Cambridge University Press, 1997)

aspect would be the quantity of speech generated and the balance of the speech events between different class members. Conversely, the awareness-raising nature of material based on analysing actual speaker interactions will be judged not so much by the quantity of speech the student produces

Quote 3.8   Cooking rice

Activity

The text examined in this unit was recorded in the kitchen of a family home; all the participants are members of the same family. Here are some brief conversational exchanges. Would you expect to find conversations such as this in a family kitchen?:

> A: Would you like a biscuit?
> B: I beg your pardon.
> A: Would you like a biscuit?
> B: Oh, yes please. Thank you very much.
>
> A: I didn't know you used boiling water to make rice.
> B: You don't have to use boiling water but it is reckoned to be quicker.

Write short notes explaining why you would or would not expect to find such styles of conversational exchange in the text examined in this unit.

Speakers and setting

<S 01>	female (45)
<S 02>	male (19)
<S 03>	male (46)
<S 04>	male (49)
<S 02>	is <S 01> and <S 04>'s son
<S 03>	is <S 04>'s brother

This extract takes place in <S 01>, <S 02> and <S 04>'s house. <S 03> is visiting them.

3	[4 secs]	
4	<S 02>	Will it all fit in the one?
5	<S 01>	No you'll have to do two separate ones
6	<S 03>	Right . . . what next?
7	[17 secs]	
8	<S 03>	Foreign body in there
9	<S 02>	It's the raisins
10	<S 03>	Oh is it oh it's rice with raisins is it?
11	<S 02>	⌐No no no it's not supposed to be
12		[laughs] erm
13	<S 03>	There must be a raisin for it being in there
14	<S 02>	D'you want a biscuit?
15	<S 03>	Erm
16	<S 02>	Biscuit?
17	<S 03>	Er yeah
18	[9 secs]	
19	<S 04>	All right
20	<S 03>	Yeah

```
21 [10 secs]
22 <S 04>    Didn't know you used boiling water
23 <S 02>    Pardon
24 <S 04>    Didn't know you used boiling water
25 <S 02>    Don't have to but it's erm … they reckon it's erm quicker
26 [5 secs]
27 <S 04>    Tony was saying they should have the heating on by about
             Wed
28 <S 02>    Just gonna put the er butter on
29 <S 04>    What you making Ian?
30 <S 02>    Mm
31 <S 04>    What's that?
32 <S 02>    Oh er just gonna do some rice
33 <S 04>    Mm
34 <S 02>    Doing some rice in the micro
35 <S 03>    So you put margarine with it
36 <S 02>    Pardon yeah little bit don't know why cos otherwise it'll
37 <S 03>                                              └Separate it
```

(R. Carter and M. McCarthy, *Exploring Spoken English*, Cambridge University Press, 1997)

when engaging with the tasks and examples, but the depth of their understanding of why speakers use the language they do in particular generic and social context.

The teaching of speaking as if it were a neutral skill which can be used as a vehicle for language practice or language acquisition more generally inevitably divorces the faculty from the issues of social context which influence even the smallest spoken interaction.

The related issue underpinning this is that it is significantly easier to teach speaking as if it were isolated from its users. Real speech brings real people into the classroom and with them the complex matters of class, gender, race, religion, politics and other culturally sensitive issues. Nowhere does this become more problematic than in the teaching of grammar in spoken contexts. The following section deals with this problem.

3.4   Teaching spoken grammar

3.4.1   Attitudes to spoken grammar

The attitudes to the spoken form of language expressed in Quotes 3.9 and 3.10 represent two widely differing schools of thought on the topic

> **Quotes 3.9 and 3.10** Two different perspectives on spoken grammar
>
> In spoken language grammar and vocabulary are reduced to a minimum. The words used often have special or hidden meaning born of some shared experience which an outsider would fail to grasp. The speaker makes much use of elided and slurred forms in the familiar patter of their ordinary every-day speech. Utterances are typically short and often elliptical. . . . Short and rugged homespun words are usually more powerful and expressive than elaborate and high-flown words. Constructions that occur commonly in speech are not necessarily acceptable in formal and dignified writing.
>
> (Yunzhong, 1985: 15)
>
> . . . [S]poken grammars have uniquely special qualities that distinguish them from written ones, wherever we look in our corpus, at whatever level of gram-matical category. In our work, too, we have expressed the view that language pedagogy that claims to support the teaching and learning of speaking skills does itself a disservice if it ignores what we know about the spoken language. Whatever else may be the result of imaginative methodologies for eliciting spoken language in the second-language classroom, there can be little hope for a natural spoken output on the part of language learners if the input is stubbornly rooted in models that owe their origin and shape to the written languages. Even much corpus-based grammatical insight . . . has been heavily biased towards evidence gleaned from written sources.
>
> (R. Carter and M. McCarthy, *Exploring Spoken English*, Cambridge University Press, 1997)

of speech. Both recognise the distinctive features of spoken discourse but contain markedly different value judgements about the implications of those distinctive characteristics. In the case of the former there is a sense of 'high' and 'low' register being the main distinguishing feature between the spoken and written forms of language. The notion of a minimal level of structure and vocabulary, 'slurred' and elliptical forms, and common-place or everyday discourse as opposed to high-flown or literary style being the norm for speech means that it is not something to be taken as a model for correct, acceptable language use in all circumstances. In this view, therefore, although the spoken form is unique, the features that go to make up that uniqueness may not be something entirely desirable for the learner to emulate, or for the teacher to introduce into the classroom.

In the case of the second quotation, the notion of 'uniquely special qualities' of speech, and the plea for more investigation of the form in its own right, imply that it is to be viewed as at least on a par with the traditionally more prestigious written form. Moreover, far from being a rather reduced and 'low' form of language the spoken form is presented as

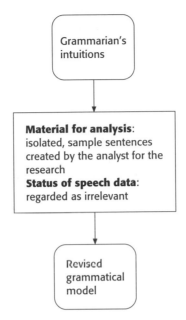

Figure 3.1   Spoken data in theoretically oriented models of grammar

having a rich and diverse grammar of its own. In this school of thought, then, the spoken form is a neglected source of subtle language choices for the learner, and a form needing to be brought closer to the heart of language descriptions and into the 'menu' of language choices made available to learners (see also Figures 3.1 and 3.2).

3.4.2   The 'ideology' of teaching spoken grammar

In teaching and researching speech one cannot get away from ideology of some kind, and the two different approaches noted above represent the end points of a continuum of attitudes about the spoken form. On the one hand teaching forms which are unique to the spoken form are seen as a marginal activity, rather as idioms or colloquialisms are often introduced into the syllabus – something to enliven a lesson, but not regarded as an essential part of a student's structural knowledge. On the other hand the spoken form is seen as a neglected source of richly diverse language choices which should be central to the teacher's repertoire of vocabulary and grammar structures to teach.

These divergent views in turn relate to more fundamental questions of language theory and the role of actual, situated linguistic data in models of language. While the ideas expressed by Yunzhong (1985) epitomise many traditional pedagogues' views of the spoken form, particularly those outside the European structuralist-influenced approaches to language, they

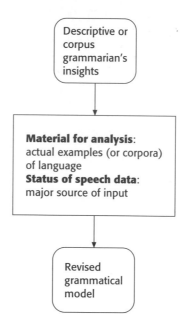

Figure 3.2 Spoken data in descriptively oriented models of grammar

also chime in with many theoretical linguists implicit denigration of the spoken form. In the case of the latter this is through a mistrust of the theoretical usefulness of actual instantiations of language as opposed to more regular underlying faculties or systems. As noted in the previous chapters, the spoken form is frequently seen as the clearest instance of 'performance' type data, because of its being so subject to the vagaries of individual user and particular contexts.

3.4.3   The question of standardisation

A further, related, thread of discussion which needs to be considered when investigating structural choices of speakers is that of target language forms and standardisation. These are important issues for applied linguistics, but they are, however, never clearer than when teaching the grammar of speech is pursued.

As long as grammar is viewed as an abstract system, represented somewhere deep in the internal 'wiring' of the human brain, then the teaching of grammar can be carried out with very little reference to data from the target form. Indeed, actual instances of contextualised language use are seen as unhelpful or of little relevance. In terms of theories of language, the standard against which a particular instance of a sample of language is judged is dependent on the intuitions of a native speaker about correctness.

Equally influential, however, is another kind of standard, when language use is judged against models of correctness influenced by historical and cultural pressures (for example the dominance of a particular dialect from the south of England which has traditionally been held in high esteem as 'standard English').

There is an understandable tendency for learners to want to acquire (and probably the majority of language teachers world-wide to teach) high-prestige forms of the language they are learning or at the very least the language of an educated minority. Whatever the political correctness of this may be, it remains a strong factor which influences syllabus design and attitudes to what is appropriate for incorporation in terms of grammatical description and course-book design.

3.4.4   The issue of idiolect

As soon as real speakers in real interactions and in socially and culturally diverse situations are taken into account in models of language, some kind of assessment needs to be made as to how far the features found are universal in the spoken form and to what extent they are particular to that speaker or that context. In this sense descriptive linguistics meets up rather interestingly with conventional language theories. This is an area which has been under-researched during a phase of rapid improvement in the descriptions of spoken forms and greater emphasis on its importance in the curriculum. There is, therefore, a great deal of opportunity for fruitful research projects in the area of both descriptive studies of spoken forms and more theoretically informed work on how far one can generalise from these studies.

3.4.5   How far can descriptive models be integrated into teaching materials

A further distinct avenue of particular interest to the classroom practitioner is the question of how far one would want actually to incorporate any generalisations about spoken forms into the syllabus as an individual teacher or into course components at an institutional level.

In general, the tendency to see the grammatical faculty at such an abstract level has permitted the majority of us to continue to teach via models of grammar which are extremely traditional, and strongly influenced by historically 'high-prestige' standard forms. These forms, as noted by McCarthy and Carter in the quotation given at the start of this section, tend to be closer to the norms of published writing than of casual speech. However, with the growing body of evidence about the grammar of speech, the individual teacher or teacher trainer may soon need to decide where they stand on the issue of how, and how far, to incorporate descriptive linguistics into their teaching.

The issues of target language are of particular interest in relation to the present section, and those which are particularly relevant in thinking about the structure and vocabulary of spoken forms are outlined here:

- What dialect form shall I teach?
- What model of correctness, if any, will I use?
- What model of pragmatic or cultural behaviour will I use?

There is little difficulty in taking real speech data as the material for listening classes, or using actual examples of interaction (for example, in student seminars) as indicative models for awareness raising of pragmatic issues among learners. More contentious, and ideologically charged, issues arise when real instances of the spoken form are taken seriously as grammatical models for the target language.

Would you, for example, teach the following to your students if they were learning English? If you were learning a language would you want to learn similar expressions in the target language?

1. 'ain't',
2. 'bloomin' thing',
3. 't'window' (instead of 'the window),
4. 'the man I told you about, his brother's wife's bought my car',
5. 'good job you told me',
6. 'he's a nice man, Harry is'.

Each of the examples given above are more typically found in the spoken form than the written. However, they exemplify different types of features, some of which are traditionally excluded from the standard language teaching syllabus, for instance forms which are felt to mark uneducated or colloquial speech such as 'ain't'. Equally, informal expressions such as 'bloomin' thing' while recognised as existing have not normally been felt appropriate for extensive teaching, other than as fairly minor adjuncts to standard grammar and vocabulary or needing to be glossed over in a listening comprehension. Finally forms which cluster together to form the dialects of geographically distinct regions, such as the use of 't'' in place of 'the' in parts of the north of England are again well known, but generally excluded from all but specialist courses.

The final three items in the list are examples of the type of feature described by Carter and McCarthy (1995) 'Grammar and the spoken language' in which the authors suggest a number of forms which are very common in speech but under-described in previous grammatical models. This kind of work is discussed in more detail in the following section. However, the question at this point is whether these forms are the kind which a teacher would want to teach their students and if so in what context.

3.4.6   Are teachers and researchers interested in the same facts about speech?

At the start of the twenty-first century the field of applied linguistics is in an exciting state of flux over its attitudes to the spoken form and, in particular, spoken grammar. It will take some time for the teaching profession to evaluate the multitude of novel ideas about speech which the work of corpus linguists and discourse analysts is throwing up. As I implied above the fact that a structure is commonly found in the spoken form of a language does not necessarily make it appropriate for language classrooms and materials. This raises the issue of whether there are differences between the focus and interest of the descriptive linguist and the classroom teacher and the question of the relationship between research and classroom materials in language teaching. Since, even when there is a relatively stable knowledge base and set of shared terminology as in traditional grammar, there are clearly differences of interest and focus between a research community and a teaching community.

This 'gap' can be widened when cutting-edge research into a dynamic and socially influenced medium such as speech is being carried out, as the applied linguistic community needs time to absorb information and judge the status of the insights before incorporating them into a syllabus. That is to say, at a certain point the teaching community will judge whether structures such as 'he's a nice man, Harry is' or 'good job you told me' (examples of a structural 'tail' and subject + verb ellipsis respectively) have the status of core grammatical features or of less central or simply less widely useful forms such as 'ain't' or 'bloomin thing'.

3.5   Perspectives on pronunciation and fluency

Quote 3.11 Byrne on oral fluency

The main goal in teaching the productive skill of speaking will be oral fluency. This can be defined as the ability to express oneself intelligibly... reasonably accurately and without too much hesitation (otherwise communication may break down because the listener loses interest or gets impatient). To attain this goal, you will have to bring the students from the stage where they are mainly imitating a model of some kind, or responding to cues, to the point where they can use the language freely to express their own ideas.

(Byrne, 1986: 9–10)

The teaching of pronunciation is something of a 'poor relation' among course components. For example, McDonough and Shaw's (1993) *Materials and Methods in ELT* contains only four brief references to the topic. Don Byrne's (1986) highly influential and much used *Teaching Oral English* contains no material on pronunciation work; and neither does Bygate's (1987) *Speaking* (still one of the few books dedicated entirely to this skill), although the latter does have some discussion on the topic of fluency/accuracy.

This final aspect brings us to the link between teaching pronunciation and broader issues of language teaching raised so vigorously (not to say contentiously) by Hector Hammerly (1991) in his book *Fluency* and [sic] *Accuracy*, a flavour of which is given in Quote 3.12. Just as explicit grammar teaching has always been carried out, and been very popular with many teachers, despite being unfashionable in current language teaching

---

Quote 3.12 Hammerly on the problems of the communicative approach in relation to accuracy

With its emphasis on communication, [the communicative approach] stresses early vocabulary development while largely ignoring language structure, whether it be phonological, morphological or syntactic. Most second-language-acquisition-through-classroom-communication/interaction advocates do not seem to care that students mispronounce sounds, use wrong stems or endings, or construct sentences following faulty rules – all of these problems are supposed to disappear, eventually, through communicative classroom interaction. Well, there is no reason why they should, and it is clear that most don't.

(Hammerly, 1991: 9)

Quote 3.13 Ur on accents

It needs to be said at the outset that the aim of pronunciation improvement is not to achieve a perfect imitation of a native accent, but simply to get the learner to pronounce accurately enough to be easily and comfortably comprehensible to other (competent) speakers. 'Perfect' accents are difficult if not impossible for most of us to achieve in a foreign language anyway, and may not even be desirable. Many people – even if subconsciously – feel they wish to maintain a slight mother-tongue accent as an assertion of personal or ethnic identity.

(Ur, 1996: 52)

> ### Quote 3.14 Lennon on impressions of fluency
>
> There is also some evidence that learning background may affect the sort of fluency behavior a learner manifests. Shin (1989) studied two learners of Japanese at similar proficiency levels at a British university. Both were native speakers of English. Subject A had spent only a few months in Japan whereas Subject B had been born in Japan and had lived there until aged 12 years. Subject A had six years of formal study of Japanese, and Subject B only three years, however. To Shin (a native speaker of Japanese), Subject B appeared the more fluent in conversation. Analysis revealed she used more colloquial forms than did Subject A, longer sentences, fewer and more appropriate fillers and fewer repetitions. Although Subject A actually paused less than did Subject B, Subject B's pause positioning seemed more appropriate. Interestingly, Subject B actually made more mistakes than did Subject A, but corrected fewer of them. In particular, she tended to let her grammatical mistakes go quite uncorrected.
>
> (Lennon, 1990: 398)

methodology, the teaching of pronunciation and more broadly 'fluency' skills have persisted largely unchanged over the last twenty years.

A comparison of the treatment of the topic in two canonical teacher-training manuals separated by nearly twenty years – Rivers and Temperly (1978) and Ur (1996) – suggests that the fundamentals have changed barely at all, and that approaches to teaching these overt speaking skills generally revolve around awareness-raising activities based on phonemic distinctions and practice based on models of correct pronunciation. While the earlier book speaks unashamedly of the remedial work needed to correct a 'foreign accent' (original scare quotes) the later work is more circumspect on this topic (see Quotes 3.15 and 3.16).

Nonetheless, the basics of pronunciation teaching remain firmly at odds with much of the ideology of modern teaching theory in that there can be seen a strong focus on external models, practice and 'getting it right'.

The above does not imply that research into speech production is moribund. In fact, the building blocks of data in the domain of pronunciation work – sounds ('phones'), meaningful sound segments ('phonemes') and the prosodic features of intonation – all lend themselves rather well to quantitative-style research projects. However, there needs to be further work to bridge the gap between these research findings and classroom practices and the induction of new practitioners in pronunciation teaching on core teacher-training programmes. Martha Pennington's work has addressed this question over the years, and has argued for a more integrated

Quotes 3.15 and 3.16 The fundamentals of teaching pronunciation in the 1970s and 1990s

The sounds we make are *phones*. Although the number of phones that can be produced by any individual speaker is practically unlimited, only certain sounds are recognised by the speakers and hearers of the particular language as conveying meaning. The smallest unit of significant or distinctive sound has been called a *phoneme*. A phoneme is actually an abstraction rather than a concrete description of a specific sound. Any particular phoneme comprises a group or class of sounds that are phonetically similar but whose articulations vary according to their position relative to the other sound which precede or follow them.

(Rivers and Temperley, 1978: 149)

The first thing that needs to be done is to check that the learner can hear and identify the sounds you want to teach. The same goes for intonation, rhythm and stress: can the learner hear the difference between how a competent, or native, speaker of the language says a word, phrase or sentence and how a foreign learner says it?

This can be done by requesting imitation; or seeing if learners can distinguish between minimal pairs (such as ship/sheep, man/men, thick/tick; see Gimson, 1978); or by contrasting acceptable with unacceptable pronunciation through recordings or live demonstration.

(Ur, 1996: 53)

and discourse-based approach to teaching pronunciation, see for example Pennington and Richards (1986) and Pennington (forthcoming)

For the teacher, the most obvious impetus to find out more about pronunciation and fluency is the desire to help students communicate better, particularly those who may have a good level of passive knowledge of the language but little ability to express this fluently and comprehensibly. At the other end of the spectrum researchers interested in language theory may want to investigate what evidence speech errors can provide for underlying sound structures or systems. Although more holistic or communicative approaches to teaching pronunciation and fluency may have been developed over the last twenty years or so, as noted in the opening of this section this is an area of language pedagogy which has changed remarkably little over the years. The central tools for the teacher remain the phonemic chart, discrimination of minimal pairs and practice based on models. Nowadays the practice may take place via a game rather than a dialogue or a drill, but the fundamentals are barely changed.

3.6   Bringing the skills together

In this chapter I have separated out the different aspects which go to make up spoken discourse in order to describe them systematically. It is, however, salutary to remember how skilful the competent speaker of any language is, and the multitude of tasks which have to be carried out simultaneously for talk to occur. Quote 3.17 gives a clear reminder of this, and realising the complexity of the skill of speaking can help build confidence for teachers and learners in approaches to spoken language.

Quote 3.17   Florez on what a good speaker does

Speakers must be able to anticipate and then produce the expected patterns of specific discourse situations. They must also manage discrete elements such as turn-taking, rephrasing, providing feedback or redirecting (Burns and Joyce, 1997).... Other skills and knowledge that instruction might address include the following:

- producing the sounds, stress patterns, rhythmic structure, and intonations of the language;
- using grammar structures accurately;
- assessing characteristics of the target audience, including shared knowledge or shared points of reference, status and power relations of participants, interest levels, or differences in perspectives;
- selecting vocabulary that is understandable and appropriate for the audience, the topic being discussed, and the setting in which the speech act occurs;
- applying strategies to enhance comprehensibility, such as emphasizing key words, rephrasing or checking for listener comprehension;
- using gestures or body language; and
- paying attention to the success of the interaction and adjusting components of speech such as vocabulary, rate of speech, and complexity of grammar structures to maximize listener comprehension and involvement. (Brown, 1994)

(Florez, 1999)

3.7   Summary

This chapter has looked at the skill of speaking from three different perspectives and addressed the central questions of how far it is possible to teach 'real' speech, the influence of context on speaker choices, and what our expectations are when we teach fluency and pronunciation. Underlying each of these issues is the core question of how much we really know about the spoken form of any target language.

Further reading

Harmer, J. (2001). *The Practice of English Language Teaching*. Harlow: Longman. (Chapters 17 and 19 deal with teaching productive skills and speaking respectively.)

Wilson, P. (2000). *Mind the Gap: ellipsis and stylistic variation in spoken and written English*. Harlow: Longman. (Chapter 9 deals explicitly with ellipsis in the spoken mode and the rest of the book with wider questions of language choices in context.)

Pica, T., Lincoln-Porter, F., Panino, D. and Linell, J. (1996). Language learners' interaction: how does it address the input, output and feedback needs of language learners?, *Tesol Quarterly*, 30/1: 59–84. (Gives a classroom-oriented overview of some of the issues in the input debate using learners' interaction as a basis for the discussion.)

Tsui, A. B. M. (1994). *English Conversation*. Oxford: Oxford University Press. (Provides a good level of detailed discussion on conversation, and an extended description using discourse analytical techniques and is particularly interesting on the differences between UK and US approaches.)

Chapter 4

Issues in assessing speaking

This chapter will ...

- discuss the key issues underlying the assessment of speaking;
- describe and compare some of the speaking components of internationally recognised oral tests of English;
- discuss the question of how far oral skills lend themselves to existing test paradigms and whether this is a problem.

4.1 Introduction

Underhill's statement in Quote 4.1 that in a genuine oral test 'real people meet face to face, and talk to each other' (Underhill, 1987: 3) summarises one of the core issues in assessing speaking. Fundamentally, speaking is an interactive, interpersonal process which does not lend itself easily to the requirements of test designers. A meaningful test of language proficiency rests on how objective, reduplicable and reliably consistent through time it is for comparative purposes. Furthermore, despite many advances in the field of language testing since Underhill's comments from the late 1980s, I will be arguing in this chapter that there remains some ambiguity in the applied linguistics profession as to whether we are testing 'speaking proficiency' or 'language proficiency'.

The nature of speech means that the potential for subjectivity, variation in test facets and, due to these two factors, difficulty in maintaining consistency across tests are far higher in the spoken form than the written. In this perhaps lies the answer to Underhill's question, 'Why have oral tests generally received little attention?' (Underhill, 1987: 3). As there are so

Quote 4.1   Underhill on the issue of what is being tested

Why have oral tests generally received little attention? Many books have been written about language testing. They follow the changing fashions of language teaching, but they usually make the same basic assumptions about the nature of language testing. Generally, little space is devoted to oral testing compared to testing the other skills. This is partly because of the difficulty of treating oral tests in the same way as other more conventional tests.

   The most striking assumption in these books is that it is the test itself that is important, while the human beings who take the test, and those who mark it, seem less important. Tests are seen as objects with an identity and a purpose of their own – you can see many references in the literature to the 'test instrument' – while the learners are often remote figures who are only of interest for their reactions to this instrument. . . . The number of possible ways they can react is strictly limited. Similarly, the preference for easily marked, multiple-choice or limited-response tests reduces markers to the role of machines. . . . In a genuine oral test, this order of priorities is reversed. Real people meet face to face, and talk to each other.

(Underhill, 1987: 3)

Quotes 4.2 and 4.3   A classroom-oriented and a more theoretical assessment of a key problem in assessing speech data

Because oral communication involves the negotiation of meaning between two or more persons, it is always related to the context in which it occurs. Speaking means negotiating intended meanings and adjusting one's speech to produce the desired effect on the listener.

(O'Malley and Pierce, 1996: 59)

The spoken performances of the test takers must be rated in some way. It is almost axiomatic that, because language use is a multicomponential phenomenon, requiring interlocutors to negotiate meanings, no two listeners hear the same message. This aspect of language use is a source of bias in test scores. It leads language test developers to severely limit which features of a performance they require raters to attend to in making their ratings. They hope that, if raters focuss attention only on pronunciation, grammar, fluency and comprehensibility, for example, the many other features of the discourse will not influence them. There is mounting evidence that this is a vain hope.

(Douglas, 1997: 22)

many competing factors which can affect speech production under test conditions – from health of the candidate to cultural expectations about how a conversation works – test designers have tended to focus on the more quantifiable aspects of language production (for example, number of errors per stretch of speech) and to constrain the test procedure to such an extent that the question of whether 'speaking' is the real focus of the test becomes an issue.

The assessment of speaking is also closely related to the issues raised in the previous chapter. O'Malley and Pierce (1996), for example, argue that test and instruction should go hand in hand and that transparent assessment criteria need to be woven into the syllabus and taken into account at the level of lesson planning. However, as with the problem of the inclusion of real people and real speech contexts in materials and classrooms, the dynamic, personal orientation of key aspects of speaking raises two crucial issues for assessment.

The first question is how far the test is a test of speaking (as opposed to more general language proficiency measured by structural complexity or accuracy of language which happens to be produced via the spoken medium). The second is the bigger question of the extent to which the characteristics of natural spoken discourse can ever lend themselves to existing assessment paradigms.

Once the language produced during a test is seen not simply as a sample of language but of communication between human beings, several serious questions are raised for the test designer. These include:

- how far the test is designed to assess ability to communicate versus linguistic knowledge;
- how far the test conditions affect the capacity for natural interaction to occur;
- how far the cultural expectations of the learner either in terms of spoken communication in the target language (or indeed between the learners involved in any interactive test) affect performance in the test;
- how far personal or psychological factors affect oral performance under test conditions;
- how far the raters' own expectations affect their judgement of oral communication.

All these questions are particularly crucial if authentic oral skills are to be tested. These are in addition the standard issues, such as rater objectivity, the need for explicit criteria for assessment, or sensitivity of test content in terms of topic, which will hold for all well-designed language tests. This begins to highlight some of the complexity surrounding oral testing.

> **Quote 4.4** Douglas on the problem of what to test in speech assessment
>
> Another aspect of the knowledge component that has implications for test development is the division of language knowledge into four subcomponents: grammatical knowledge, textual knowledge, illocutionary knowledge, and sociolinguistic knowledge. The question is whether a speaking test, or a test of any of the language skills, should test each of the four areas. That is, should there be test sections, items, or tasks that require the testee to display ability in each knowledge subcomponent, or should such differentiation be a part of the scoring/rating procedure (on the assumption that all four areas are 'in play' all the time in communication)? Before an answer can be given to this question, much more research is needed on the nature of language knowledge and the interaction among its components.
>
> (Douglas, 1997: 14)

4.2 Language proficiency versus speaking proficiency

A first key question in the assessment of speaking should, therefore, perhaps be the teasing out of the concept of 'language proficiency' versus 'conversational', 'spoken language' or 'discourse' proficiency.

Testing processes are founded on test criteria. Whether carried out via an external observer/rater, an interactive examiner, or self-assessment test, performance is held up against a set of beliefs about 'better' or 'worse' or

> **Quote 4.5** Johnson and Tyler on preconceptions about conversation
>
> ...[O]ne of the central characteristics of naturally occurring conversation... is that language users are largely unaware of how conversation is typically structured and managed. When asked to articulate conversational practices, native-speaker pronouncements are often at odds with what speakers actually do (Wolfson, 1989). Much of how everyday conversation works is so deceptively familiar that people studying and testing language often overlook fundamental characteristics of conversation.
>
> (Johnson and Tyler, 1998: 27)

'more effective' or 'weaker' language use. Crucial in this area therefore is the state of knowledge (and beliefs or preconceptions) about speech and how this relates to a fundamental question in assessing speaking: what is regarded as good or appropriate speech?

A key aspect of naturally occurring spontaneous speech is that interolocutors do not focus on the mechanics of their interaction but on the ideas/emotions/information being conveyed. The nature of language testing means that a strong focus tends to be put on the actual samples of language used: their range, variety, complexity, or accuracy in relation to pre-decided criteria. This is a primary cause of tension between test design criteria and natural oral production. Speaking is not naturally language focused, rather it is people focused. Language testing is not naturally people focused but by its nature will tend to be language focused. To give an example, many native speakers are extremely hesitant in their speech delivery, particularly when being asked to do something such as form an opinion 'on the hoof'. However, the listener will not tend to notice the pausing, um-ing and er-ing in their interest to hear the answer to their question or the opinion of the speaker.

Here is an example of a university student trying to express an opinion:

> The plan was always . . . [−*pause*]. The plan was never to let go but to er assimilate em the Africans into er sort of wider France [inaudible] or whatever was to er assimilate the Africans into a larger France, never to sort of . . . like Britain. The plan was, I mean they saw an end to the road, they never said they would hold on to it.
>
> (Carter and McCarthy, 1997: 137)

This (male) student had already given a presentation on the topic of 'Does France need Africa as much as Africa needs France?' in a politics seminar and had therefore had time to think about the central concepts and opinions he held. However, set against oral proficiency criteria which require the ability to 'form coherent monologue' (UCLES, 2000b: 75), 'express ideas and opinions in coherent, connected speech' (UCLES, 2000a: 56) or which focus on 'the range of vocabulary the candidate can use and the precision with which meaning and attitudes can be expressed' IELTS, 2001: 15) this native speaker of English would not fare particularly well.

Spontaneous interactive speech will be full of hesitations, false-starts, grammatical inaccuracies, have a limited vocabulary, tend towards repetition and be structured around short thought units or quasi-clauses based on the constraints of breath and of spoken language processing. It takes a considerable change in preconceptions about language proficiency for, for example, single word answers to be regarded as 'good'.

Quote 4.6 Riggenbach on the problem of preconceptions about speech

Conversation with friends calls for common, simple, familiar vocabulary. When students in my third year undergraduate/junior level 'Introduction to Language Studies' course at the University of Washington first listen in depth to an excerpt of dinner table conversation involving four native speaker adults, their first impressions often include descriptions of the native speakers as uneducated, based, in part, on their simple, unremarkable vocabulary usage.

This impression also applies to native speaker fluency. For novice conversation analyses, the amount of repair, hesitation, and lack of smoothness in normal native speaker conversation comes as something of a shock. Traditional definitions of fluency – reflected in rating scales designed to assess non-native speaker speech such as the Test of Spoken English – include phrases such as 'smoothness of speech,' 'effortlessness', and 'speech exhibiting automaticity'... Typical native speaker speech in conversation is often lacking in these qualities.

(Riggenbach, 1998: 63–64)

4.3   The issue of interactivity

A further fundamental aspect of testing oral skills is the issue of interactivity and the effects this facet of natural spoken discourse has in terms of the ability to assess speaking. Fundamentally, if you are speaking with someone with whom you are 'on the same wavelength', communication will be easier than with someone with whom you feel you have little in common.

Quote 4.7 Butler *et al.* on the issue of test conditions and interactivity

It is important to recognize that a test imposes certain constraints on the character of the interactions that are created in the assessment and thus on the validity of generalizations from performances on the test to performance in ordinary interactions outside the test. Success in spoken interaction is determined by (a) the nature of the tasks that the interaction requires and the roles in that interaction; (b) the conditions under which the participants are required to perform; and (c) the resources the individual brings to the interaction.

(Butler *et al.*, 2000: 2)

Whether a candidate is asked to interact with an examiner or with another student, the interactive nature of speech and the level of personal involvement which even formal speaking will lead to mean that it is extremely hard to eliminate the effects of one speaker on another. This is in part due to the fact that good oral communication is founded on one speaker actually having an effect on another, and on the reactions and responses which take place between interlocutors.

The more constrained the response types and contexts (for example, assessment through a taped utterance in response to a recorded prompt) the more neutral and objective the test process would therefore appear to be. In the case of the Educational Testing Service researched tests of speaking that were current at the time of writing both the TSE (Test of Spoken English) and the SPEAK test (Speaking Proficiency English Assessment Kit) required response to taped prompts from an examiner on a range of tasks and functions within 30 to 90 seconds.

However, this returns us to the questions of authenticity and validity in terms of what the models for rating performance in oral tests actually are. These are questions for all language test designers, but, due to the poor state of knowledge and understanding of what it is to be a good or bad speaker in one's first language, the question of assessing spoken discourse proficiency is more pressing than in many cases. The testing of listening skills is another area which has a similar range of difficult problems surrounding the question of what is actually being tested and how far test conditions constrain performance (see also Rost, 2002).

4.4 The issue of creating authentic conditions for speech testing

The issue of authenticity of what is being tested rests on two main factors. The first is how far any spoken test event can mimic authentic speech contexts. Douglas (1997) sees the challenge as 'to consider how test methods can be manipulated to engage features of natural spoken discourse' or at least take into account which features of the test takers spoken performance are a result of the test method being used. This, however, is problematic.

The reason why this may not be straightforward is that the individual, inter-personal and cultural factors which affect speech performance, whether in test or non-test conditions (and whether in one's own language or a target language) are little understood.

This leads us to the second main question underlying authenticity in oral testing. Authentic speech tasks require considerable specification of

Quote 4.8 Douglas on the problem of natural spoken discourse under test conditions

In implementing new test delivery methods, developers must take into account their effects on the nature of the discourse of responses. The challenge is to consider how test methods can be manipulated to engage features of natural spoken discourse, or at least to control for those produced by the method facets. For example, instructions should be designed to give test takers plausible reasons for carrying out the required speaking tasks; the input format should be dialogic to the degree possible; the discourse in the input and expected response should be context embedded (i.e. contain linguistic, paralinguistic, and situational cues) and spoken genre should be employed containing grammatical, cohesive and rhetorical features of spoken discourse. ... The relationship between the input and the expected response should be reciprocal; that is, the speaker's message should have the capability of reducing uncertainty in the listener, which in turn will allow the listener to fashion a message in response that reflects the change in information. Thus, there should be provision for the test taker to formulate a communicative goal or intention and to see that goal affect the interlocutor.

(Douglas, 1997: 21–22)

goals and context. As soon as one moves from a relatively neutral task, such as 'giving directions', issues of topics and tasks being biased in favour of one set of test takers over another emerge. In addition, even such an apparently neutral process as responding to the taped prompt – 'I'd like to see a movie. Please give me directions from the bus station to the movie theater' (ETS practice question) – together with a visual prompt of a map of a town is not as straightforward as it seems.

The advantage of this task is that the aural and visual stimuli remain rigorously the same for all test takers and, given the impersonality of the test procedure, differences due to inter-personal factors will be minimised. Thus the comparability of candidate responses is higher than in more natural interactions. However, the question is whether the response to such inauthentic stimuli can be regarded as 'authentic speech'. Rather it may be better described as the oral delivery of test-rehearsed material within a given time. More specifically this speech event by the test candidate can be characterised as the tape recording by someone of information for an unknown, non-present interlocutor who expresses a desire for entertainment via a taped recording and wants to know how to get from a place of transportation to a place of entertainment in a nameless town of which he or she knows a map exists. This inevitably begs the question of whether test-taking techniques or genuine oral skills are the object of the task.

The criteria and conditions of oral testing for taped or highly constrained speech assessment tests look particularly limited if the skills involved are compared with something like Riggenbach's breakdown of discourse competence (Riggenbach, 1998) which includes the fundamental conversational ability to claim and yield turns of talk.

Quote 4.9 **Riggenbach's breakdown of discourse competence**

Some of the skills that display a learner's discourse and strategic competence in conversation are listed below. These skills, micro both in the sense of relative length and functional scale, are necessary elements in coherent, fluid turn-taking (discourse competence) and in successful negotiation of meaning in the case of potential communication breakdown (strategic competence).

Conversation micro skills

the ability to claim turns of talk

the ability to maintain turns of talk, once claimed

the ability to yield turns of talk

the ability to backchannel

the ability to self-repair

the ability to ensure comprehension on the part of the listener (e.g. comprehension checks such as *Does that make sense? Are you with me? Get it?*)

the ability to initiate repair when there is a potential breakdown (e.g. clarification requests)

the ability to employ compensatory strategies (e.g. avoidance of structures or vocabulary beyond the learner's proficiency, word coinage, circumlocution, and even shifting topics or asking questions that stimulate the other interlocutor to share the responsibility for maintaining the conversation flow).

(Riggenbach, 1998: 57)

The counter-argument to criticisms of highly constrained oral test conditions is that there may be a correlation between test performance and genuine speaking skills. That is to say, although there is an inevitable mismatch between the test criteria and conditions and naturally occurring speech the test may still give an accurate indication of speaking ability. A number of TOEFL research papers have been produced which suggest this to be the case. For instance Sarwak *et al.* (1995) found that the oral performance in class of teaching assistants correlated well with their performance in the SPEAK test (this is a highly desirable finding as the test is very easily administered at an institution via a 'kit' of tapes and answer key and does not require trained examiners on site). These questions of oral performance in and outside constrained test conditions would be a highly interesting area for further research, and I suggest one such project in Chapter 8.

4.5   The issue of spoken genres and testing

Concept 4.1 Field-specific tests

Field-specific oral tests relate to the testing of speech genres, but are a more well-established concept in the literature of assessment. Some professional contexts require very specific oral language use (for example, air traffic control; doctor–patient encounters) and tests can be constructed which are designed to assess the test takers ability to communicate in relation to typical language of these target genres.

A further issue in oral assessment relates to the question of what speech genres, if any, are being tested, and of 'field-specific' or specific purpose tests versus general tests. These are discussed in greater detail in Dan Douglas's book *Assessing Languages for Specific Purposes* (Douglas, 2000).

In the case of speech genres there is growing evidence to suggest that the language choices made by speakers are strongly influenced by the genre of talk they are participating in. For example, the densely informative (and therefore noun-phrase packed) monologue of a seminar presentation versus the less densely structured conversational content which takes place during 'language-in-action' or service encounters.

However, much more work is needed if the oral test designer is to be able to construct test conditions in which realistic speech genres can be produced; and if test criteria are to be matched more closely to real speech data. In addition the extensive training of raters would also be essential. As noted above, it takes a change of mind-set to realise that hesitancy, short clauses (or even single word turns), ellipsis, repetitions, self-repair and simple or inexplicit vocabulary may be the essence of excellent speech

Quote 4.10   Underhill on the importance of the context and purpose of an oral test

You need full local knowledge. Tests are not inherently good or bad, valid or invalid; they become so when they are applied to a particular situation. You cannot say how good a hand-tool is unless you know exactly what it is used for; similarly, you can only evaluate a test in a specific context.

(Underhill, 1987: 6)

production in certain conversational genres. In contrast, long turns, explicit phrasing and densely structured talk may be found in spoken narrative. This is why the issue of speech genres would need to be taken into account in relation to 'authentic' oral testing.

Quotes 4.11 and 4.12 Two views on the role and influence of test methods

While it is generally recognized that [specification of the task or test domain] involves the specification of the ability domain, what is often ignored is that examining content relevance also requires the specification of the test method facets.

(Bachman, 1990: 244)

Rather than attempting to minimize the effects of test method facets on the interpretation of results, testers should use them to design tests for particular populations.

(Douglas, 1997: 18)

4.6 Integrated versus discrete skills testing

Another issue in the testing of oral skills is the degree to which it is possible to isolate speech from other skills in test design. This is known as the distinction between integrated versus discrete skills testing. The question arises in all language testing, for example the degree to which reading ability influences performance in a written test; however, the matter is particularly interesting in relation to the testing of aural/oral skills.

Quote 4.13 Douglas on the issue of integrated or discrete testing of speaking skills

At present, however, it seems to me that listening and speaking are theoretically and practically very difficult to separate. I recommend that serious consideration be given to integrating them, both methodologically and psychometrically. That is, I believe we should consider an oral/aural skills test, where the test taker uses his or her communicative language ability to produce and comprehend meanings in a variety of tasks and receives a single score reflecting the performance.

(Douglas, 1997: 25–26)

Douglas (1997) argues that the theoretical and practical difficulties of teasing out listening and speaking from one another in test design means that a single test of both skills is desirable.

However, I would argue that a more radical view is that it is only our present, very 'literate', conceptualisation of language which brings us to the position where we consider it feasible to test discrete language skills in any meaningful sense. The presence of the individually produced written text, such as the exam. essay, which persists through time as a discrete object for analysis by assessors, encourages us to believe that all aspects of language can be tested in this assessment-friendly way. I suggest that in language testing it may be refreshing (and possibly fruitful) to regard writing as the exception and that the assessment of the dynamic and inter-personal skills of speaking and listening (and, to an extent, also reading) have tended to be constrained and defined by the norms of the written mode.

4.7   A comparison of test paradigms for oral assessment

The difficulty of moving from a test paradigm which does not lend itself readily to inter-personal skills towards a more holistic framework can be seen in the long birth pangs of new 'communicative' language tests which at the time of writing were in the process of being finalised and launched globally by the University of Cambridge Local Examinations Syndicate (UCLES). These are the Certificates in English Language Skills (CELS) tests which have been under development since the early 1980s and were brought about by an amalgamation under one umbrella of two competing schemes (the UCLES 'Certificates in Communicative use of English' (CCSE) and the Oxford EFL examinations).

It will be interesting to see how these task-oriented and inter-personal tests fare in competition with the more traditional skills-based inter-national tests, such as IELTS, TOEFL and the Cambridge 'Main Suite' Examinations (UCLES FCE ('First Certificate'), CAE ('Cambridge Advanced') and CPE ('Cambridge Proficiency').

The CELS test format and focus for assessment is an example of a test framework which takes into account (or, rather, does not try to exclude from the test design) far more of the dynamic and interpersonal facets of speech communication. In addition to the aspects of assessment focus which the tests share with the 'Main Suite' examinations the test takes 'interactive communication (turn-taking, initiating and responding)' into account in the final stage of the test.

Table 4.1   **Certificates in English Language Skills' test format for speaking** (based on UCLES, 2000a: 55)

Part	Interaction pattern	Input	Function	Assessment focus
1	Candidates talk individually with interlocutor on prompts they have chosen	1 Written stimulus from task 2 Oral stimulus form interlocutor	Describing, giving opinions, giving personal information, stating (dis)likes and preferences, commenting	Grammar and vocabulary
2a	Interlocutor sets up task; candidates talk together	Written stimulus form task	(dis)agreeing, deciding, comparing, explaining, giving/exchanging opinions, negotiating, planning, giving reasons, justifying, prioritising, selecting, stating (dis)likes and preferences, summarising, suggesting, persuading, commenting	Discourse management Pronunciation
2b	Three way discussion between interlocutor and candidates	Written prompt on task sheet + oral prompts from interlocutor + discussion from 2a	As for Part 2a	Interactive communication

Table 4.1 describes the test procedure for the recently re-launched communicative/skills-based tests of English – the Certificates in English Language Skills. When compared with a taped prompt–response type oral test, such as described above for TOEFL, this format, intuitively at least, demands a greater range of interactive skills to be used (individual speech, dialogue and three-way discussion) and a variety of spoken genres and registers to be produced. The disadvantage of this format and the greater unpredictability of certain aspects which it inevitably brings is that a number of other factors will creep in to affect test performance. For example, the personality and more specifically the levels of personal inter-active skills of the paired candidates, the differences in conversational expectation of paired candidates and the dynamics holding between

assessor(s) and candidates will, potentially, influence the speech produced during the test.

A highly constrained test, on the other hand, will remove many of these variables. The question remains, therefore, how far a test score obtained under such circumstances correlates to speech outside the test event.

4.8   The criteria for three tests of speaking compared

Table 4.2 compares the criteria used in three international tests of English-speaking ability. It is interesting to note first the range of criteria (two – CPE and CELS – include the topic of 'Interactive Communication' which is omitted from the IELTS test criteria), and second the differences in emphasis between the three tests. The IELTS criteria reveal the greatest explicit focus on accuracy and on quantifiable data (e.g. 'the number of grammatical errors in a given amount of speech' (IELTS, 2000: 15)). But on the whole there is a high level of consensus between the three tests (due in part, of course, to their all being from the UCLES 'stable'). For example, under grammatical criteria all three tests assess spoken performance in terms of 'accuracy' or 'range' or 'complexity'. This returns us directly to the question of whether these really are key indicators of speech proficiency in a first language and how far they should be the criteria for assessment in a second language context.

Table 4.2   **Criteria for three speaking tests**

IELTS (International English Language Testing System)

Fluency and coherence. This refers to the ability to talk with normal levels of continuity, rate and effort and to link ideas and language together to form coherent, connected speech. The key indicators of fluency are speech rate and speech continuity. The key indicators of coherence are logical sequencing of sentences, clear marking of stages in a discussion narration or argument, and the use of cohesive devices (e.g. connectors, pronouns and conjunctions) within and between sentences (IELTS, 2001: 14).

Lexical resource. This refers to the range of vocabulary the candidate can use and the precision with which meanings and attitudes can be expressed. The key indicators are the variety of words used, the adequacy and appropriacy of the words used and the ability to circumlocute (get round a vocabulary gap by using other words) with or without noticeable hesitation (IELTS, 2001: 15).

Table 4.2 *(Cont'd)*

Grammatical range and accuracy. This refers to the range and the accurate and appropriate use of the candidate's grammatical resource. The key indicators of grammatical range are the length and complexity of the spoken sentences, the appropriate use of subordinate clauses, and the range of sentence structure, especially to move elements around for information focus. The key indicators of grammatical accuracy are the number of grammatical errors in a given amount of speech and the communicative effect of error. (IELTS, 2001: 15)

Pronunciation. This refers to the ability to produce comprehensible speech to fulfil the speaking test requirements. The key indicators will be the amount of strain caused to the listener, the amount of the speech which is unintelligible and the noticeability of L1 influence (IELTS, 2001: 15).

CPE (Certificate of Proficiency in English)[a]

Discourse management. This refers to the ability to link utterances together to form coherent monologue and contributions to dialogue. The utterances should be relevant to the tasks and to preceding utterances in the discourse. The discourse produced should be at a level of complexity appropriate to CPE level and the utterances should be arranged logically to develop the themes or arguments required by the tasks. The extent of contributions should be appropriate, i.e. long or short as required at a particular point in the dynamic development of the discourse in order to achieve the task (UCLES, 2000b: 75).

Lexical resource. This refers to the candidate's ability to use a wide and appropriate range of vocabulary to meet task requirements. At CPE level the tasks require candidates to express precise meaning, attitudes and options and to be able to convey abstract ideas. Although candidates may lack specialised vocabulary when dealing with unfamiliar topics, it should not in general terms be necessary to resort to simplification (UCLES, 2000b: 75).

Grammatical resource. This refers to the accurate application of grammar rules and the effective arrangement of words in utterances. At CPE level a wide range of structures should be used appropriately and competently (UCLES, 2000b: 75).

Pronunciation. This refers to the ability to produce easily comprehensible utterances. Articulation of individual sounds is not required to be native speaker-like but should be sufficiently clear for all words to be easily understood. An acceptable rhythm of connected speech should be achieved by the appropriate use of strong and weak syllables, the smooth linking of words and the effective highlighting of information-bearing words. Intonation, which includes the use of a sufficiently wide pitch range and the appropriate use of contours, should be used effectively to convey meaning (UCLES, 2000b: 75).

Interactive communication. This refers to the ability to take an active part in the development of the discourse, showing sensitivity to turn taking and without undue hesitation. It requires the ability to participate competently in the range of interactive situations in the test and to develop discussions on a range of topics by initiating and responding appropriately. It also refers to the deployment of strategies to maintain and repair interaction at an appropriate level throughout the test so that the tests can be fulfilled (UCLES, 2000b: 75).

Table 4.2   *(Cont'd)*

CELS (Certificates in English Language Skills)

Discourse management. On this scale, examiners are looking for evidence of the candidate's ability to express ideas and opinions in coherent, connected speech. The CELS tasks require candidates to construct sentences and produce utterances (extended as appropriate) in order to convey information and to express or justify opinions. The candidates' ability to maintain a coherent flow of language with an appropriate range of linguistic resources over several utterances is assessed here (UCLES, 2000a: 56).

Grammar and vocabulary (accuracy and appropriacy). On this scale, candidates are awarded marks for the accurate and appropriate use of syntactic forms and vocabulary in order to meet the task requirements at each level. The range and appropriate use of vocabulary are also assessed here (UCLES, 2000a: 56).

Pronunciation (individual sounds and prosodic features). This refers to the candidate's ability to produce comprehensible utterances to fulfil the task requirements, i.e. the production of individual sounds, the appropriate linking of words, and the use of stress and intonation to convey the intended meaning. First language accents are acceptable provided communication is not impeded (UCLES, 2000a: 56).

Interactive communication (turn-taking, initiating and responding). This refers to the candidate's ability to interact with the interlocutor and the other candidate by initiating and responding appropriately and at the required speed and rhythm to fulfil the task requirements. It includes the ability to use functional language and strategies to maintain or repair interaction, e.g. in conversational turn-taking, and willingness to develop the conversation and move the task towards a conclusion. Candidates should be able to maintain the coherence of the discussion and may, if necessary, ask the interlocutor or the other candidate for clarification (UCLES, 2000a: 56).

Note:
[a] There are two examiners in the CPE speaking test. These are the criteria used by the observing examiner. In addition, the examiner who acts as the interlocutor gives a global score for performance throughout the test.

4.9 Summary

A number of questions surrounding oral assessment have been raised in this chapter including two central ones:

- Is speaking ability really the object of current assessment procedures or is something closer to 'language proficiency' being tested instead?
- If we had a better understanding of 'good', 'effective' or 'appropriate' speaking in different contexts, could we move towards oral test criteria which are more closely aligned to the micro-skills and structures which create speaking ability?

These questions could, in themselves, be interesting starting points for research projects into speaking proficiency. Such research, together with further work on the correlations between test performance and communicative ability outside test conditions would form a basis for answering the bigger question which is how far it is realistically possible to assess speaking from a perspective other than 'language proficiency'.

Further reading

A good initial read for background purposes would be:

Bachman, L. F. (1990). *Fundamental Considerations in Language Testing.* Oxford: Oxford University Press.

A summary of some key theoretical issues can be found in:

Douglas, D. (1997). Testing speaking ability in academic contexts: theoretical considerations. *TOEFL Monograph Series.* Princeton, NJ: Educational Testing Services.

A fuller discussion of the issue of the effects of face-to-face oral assessments versus tape-mediated tests can be found in:

O'Loughlin, K. (2001). *The Equivalence of Direct and Semi-Direct Speaking Tests.* Cambridge: Cambridge University Press.

Detailed information about the performance of test-takers in other contexts can be found in:

Sarwark, S., Smith, J., MacCullam, R. and Cascallar, E. C. (1995). *A Study of Characteristics of the SPEAK Test.* RR 94–47. Princeton, NJ: Educational Testing Service.

A people-focused balance to all the above, if a little out of date by now, is:

Underhill, N. (1987). *Testing Spoken Language: a handbook of oral testing techniques.* Cambridge: Cambridge University Press.

An interesting collection of research papers questioning the relationship between oral proficiency interviews and real spoken discourse can be found in:

Young, R. and Weiyun He, A. (1998). *Talking and Testing: discourse approaches to the assessment of oral proficiency. Studies in Bilingualism,* 14, Amsterdam and Philadelphia: John Benjamins Publishing Company.

Chapter 5

Approaches to researching speech

This chapter will...

- present summaries of case studies into various aspects of research particularly relevant to broadening our understanding of speech;
- consider the stance and research frameworks or approaches described in these projects.

5.1 Introduction

This chapter falls into three main sections. The first deals with global, higher-level features of speech and some ways these have been researched previously. The second looks at grammatical and structural choices made by speakers in context, and in particular the role of two central, and under-researched, aspects: the influence of discourse context or genre on grammatical choice and the role of mode in language processing. Finally, three research articles present different approaches to the topic of fluency and pronunciation ranging from 'standard' inter-lingual studies to less-central but exciting work on language learning (in particular spoken word-boundary discrimination) as a statistical problem.

5.2 Research into global features of speech

5.2.1 Data and experimentally oriented work on spoken discourse

This section discusses a paper called 'On the teachability of communication strategies' by Zoltan Dörnyei published in 1995 in *TESOL Quarterly*.

This paper is discussed because it deals with an issue in language teaching and learning which is particularly pertinent to the domain of speech: communication strategies. Secondly, the paper is a good example of how classical experimental or quantitative research approaches can be applied to concepts highly relevant to the teacher.

Concept 5.1   'Communication strategies'

This is a term relating to the ability of a language user actively to manipulate a conversation and negotiate interactions effectively. Such strategies are particularly beneficial when there is some difficulty of expression or communication. A classic example of such a strategy is for a language user to cope with the lack of a particular word by a variety of verbal and non-verbal means. The speaker might expand the word in a circumlocution ('Hammer' – 'a tool you use for putting nails in the wall), or represent the word non-verbally through gesture, or use an 'empty' expression such as 'whatsit', 'thing', 'thingy' or 'thingummy'.

Major issues in the field of communication strategies are how far these conversational skills will merely develop alongside other elements of language acquisition, how far in adult learners they will be simply transferred from one language to another, and the efficacy of explicit teaching in relation to them.

Dörnyei (1995) outlines the topic of communication strategies in general, describes the major problems underlying communication strategy research (and in so doing positions the author in relation to the issues), and then moves on to present a quantitatively oriented study and a statistical analysis of learners who had and had not had explicit training in communication strategies.

Quote 5.1 Dörnyei on the usefulness of communication strategies in spoken communication

Because a significant proportion of real-life L2 communication is problematic, L2 learners might benefit from instruction on how to cope with performance problems.... This article first describes what communication strategies are and provides an overview of the teachability issue, discussing the arguments for and against strategy instructions.... After this the results of a study aimed at obtaining empirical data on the educational potential of strategy training are presented. The findings point to the possibility of developing the quality and quantity of learners' use of at least some communication strategies through focused instruction.

(Dörnyei, 1995: 55)

The paper is interesting because it gives a significant amount of background discussion about the underlying problems, differences in interpretation of the key terms and the scope of them before moving on to present the quantitative, experimentally oriented material.

The level of critical evaluation of the state of work in the field in Dörnyei (1995) strengthens the overall results and pre-empts criticisms and objections to the findings by seeking to clarify exactly what is being investigated. In this paper the writer needs to clear the ground quite considerably because there are a number of critics who would suggest that the whole enterprise of teaching communication strategies is wrong headed. For example, some would argue that such oral strategies are just superficial 'performance-' related elements and not part of language competence at all.

Another argument reviewed by Dörnyei, similar in nature but different in ideology, is that training is a waste of time because the strategies are themselves indicators of a more significant underlying psychological process. Finally, the pragmatic argument against explicit communication strategy training is that learners already have awareness of such strategies in their first language, can transfer them adequately and will develop appropriate ones simply by exposure to the target language.

Before he can more on to his research questions, therefore, the author setting out to do experimentally oriented work must deal with these objections and why the current approach is an improvement on previous work. Most telling in this article is the fact that the author notes that previous arguments on both sides have been based on indirect evidence, a move which further justifies the experimentally based research being presented in the paper. That is to say, making this point works for the writer of a quantitative academic paper in two different ways: it highlights the weaknesses in previous work on the topic and points out the particular need for objective evidence – evidence which the present research will provide. This is a good example of the way in which setting out the research framework and background in a literature review or introductory section can help the academic to engage the interest of the reader.

In an experimentally oriented paper the research questions are generally presented as an explicit part of the research method. This is because in designing the experiment the researcher needs to decide what precisely is to be discovered and then how the answers are to be found. In the case of Dörnyei (1995) there are five explicit questions listed:

1. Does the training of a specific strategy increase the frequency of the use of this strategy by the students?

2. Does the training of a specific strategy improve the quality (efficiency) of this strategy in actual language use?

3. Does strategy training have a direct impact on the students' speech rate?

4. Is the success of strategy training related to the students' initial level of language proficiency?
5. What are the students' attitudes toward strategy training and the usefulness of CSs?

(Dörnyei, 1995: 66)

Points with which the reader might take issue with the design and conclusions of the research presented in Dörnyei relate interestingly to some of the limitations of the experimental approach in relation to real speech data. For example, Dörnyei states that three strategies were to be investigated – avoidance/replacement; circumlocution; and pauses/fillers – and the teaching techniques for these three areas are outlined as distinct from one another in the experimental method. Nevertheless the last two areas are given more prominence in the results and discussion than the first (avoidance/replacement). 'Avoidance' by its very nature is a difficult aspect to quantify and, in practical research terms, the design, dissemination and analysis of a questionnaire on the *quality* of students' speaking task performance can be seen to have become a major focus for the project. In the statistical analysis and the results, discussion and conclusion the actual focus is on two strategies, the most 'countable', therefore, rather than three introduced earlier. Secondly, in relation to the quality-of-use issue there is rather more attention paid to the circumlocution strategy rather than pauses/fillers. This imbalance is perhaps due to the greater ease of defining 'quality of use' in relation to circumlocution as opposed to the latter hesitation features.

It is also interesting to note that neither in this article nor in most research based on strategy training is the question of mode mentioned explicitly. Communication strategies are, as generally conceived, almost solely relevant to spoken mode. The whole question of 'buying time' to find the correct expression or of 'repairing' a stretch of language only arises when processing and production constraints are such that planning and editing of language cannot take place. These kinds of constraint are much stronger in speech than in writing. This raises the idea that there is a whole component of the language faculty (i.e. devoted to coping with the demands of on-line production and processing of language) which, a strong argument would say, is dedicated to the spoken mode. However, the current 'unitary' and 'a-modal' notions of language mean that is seems irrelevant to ask the more fundamental question of the placement, range and scope of communication strategies in the language faculty and how far they are mode sensitive.

Experimental and quantitatively oriented work on speech can have very direct relevance to the classroom. By its nature quantitative research gives a sense of objective, factual information reached by rational and reduplicable means. The classic experimental research paradigm also tends to discuss explicitly the limitations of the work and this in turn can assist the practitioner or teacher trainer when assessing the relevance of the findings to their own context. Experimentally oriented work at this global level into speech communication can also provide insights about some of the distinctive features of speech communication as opposed to the written mode and embed these within a 'real-world' context. For instance, the types of strategy described by Dörnyei assist the learner in the dynamic interactive processes of speech, and, it would seem from his conclusions, are beneficial to all levels of learner.

5.2.2   Qualitatively oriented approaches to spoken discourse

Quote 5.2   Douglas on discourse ability

Speakers want to present themselves as modest, competent, socialized beings and to attribute the same features to their interlocutors. Language/culture-specific ways of signaling [sic] these features are very much a part of what it means to know a language and to be judged a competent speaker of it. . . . Discourse ability is, therefore, an important aspect of what it means to know a language.

(Douglas, 1997: 21)

In contrast to Dörnyei's research discussed above, this section introduces research which is more qualitatively focused. The paper in question also deals with an aspect of higher-level, conversational or pragmatic facets of speech: differences in conversational style between speakers of English from different cultures. Scollon and Wong-Scollon (1991) present an analysis of possible reasons for miscommunication in English conversation between, to use their terms, 'Asian' and 'Western' speakers.

I am including this paper not only because it is a good representative example of culturally oriented, qualitative work on speech, but also it is an interesting example, in contrast to Dörnyei (1995), of the setting up of research frameworks and questions. Whereas Dörnyei uses a classical research paradigm in relation to his work on communication strategies, moving from a general question of their teachability to a set of precise research questions to be answered via an experiment and statistical analysis, Scollon and Wong-Scollon have a very different approach. Their research framework – where they are coming from in terms of underlying assumptions and methods – grows naturally from the insights of conversation analysts such as Emanuel Schegloff (1968, 1979) in the USA during the 1970s. In fact they adapt his summons–answer model, re-naming it

> **Quote 5.3**   Scollon and Wong-Scollon (1991)
>
> Abstract
>
> Most communication between Asians and Westerners takes place in English. This misleads us into believing that little translation work is required for East and West to understand each other. Nevertheless, when speakers of Chinese, Korean, and Japanese use English there is a tendency for them to introduce topics in ways which are unexpected from the point of view of English-speaking Westerners. The Asian inductive, or delayed, introduction of topics leaves Westerners confused about what the topic is. Conversely, Westerners introduce topics early in a conversation. This deductive pattern strikes the Asian as abrupt or rude while the Asian pattern tends to feel evasive or 'inscrutable' to the Westerner. Since these patterns of topic introduction are largely unconscious, conversants are not able to locate the source of their confusion in the discourse structure and so have the tendency to blame their conversants. Some of the stereotypical attitudes of East and West toward each other can be shown to be the direct outcome of these unconsciously differing discourse practices in the introduction of topics.
>
> (Scollon and Wong-Scollon, 1991: 113)

call-answer and introduce their own work via a discussion of the classical studies on patterns of topic initiation.

However, what is noticeable in contrast to more traditional research paradigms is the tendency here, as for the majority conversation analysts, to base judgements simply on their own interpretations of the data and to see no problem in generalising from these. This approach is founded on providing compelling descriptive insights rather than objective investigative rigour and as such does not value so highly the precisely formulated research question. In this it shares considerable ground with ethnographic approaches to the study of speaking or of teaching speaking.

Therefore, whereas you could begin from a general question such as 'why is there sometimes confusion in conversation between Asian and Western speakers of English?', or 'what causes confusion in . . . ?' (or, more fundamentally, 'is there confusion in . . . ?') and investigate the possible reasons via a series of carefully constructed research questions, this paper follows an overall problem–explanation form.

The problem is regarded as a given (summed up in the title of the paper 'Topic confusion in English–Asian discourse') and the explanation is based on a series of generalisations expanded on in relation to basic conversational differences, conversation in different contexts (friends/acquaintances/family versus strangers/service encounters) and the implications of the differences for education, business, government and so on.

The insights are intuitively persuasive. The fundamental point made is that while East and West share some conversational characteristics in that they begin with the 'call–answer' pattern, the Western discourse model requires a statement of the purpose of the conversation, or the topic, early on in the conversation, typically by the person who made the initial call.

Classic call–answer patterns in US or UK conversation:

A: Summons or call   'Hi'
B: Answer   'Hi'
A: Introduction of topic 'Are you doing anything tonight?'

Scollon and Wong-Scollon contrast this with a pattern they suggest is more typical of Asian discourse. This model begins with a call–answer, but then a period of 'small-talk' or 'facework' is engaged in before the topic is introduced. In some instances, if the small-talk suggests that the moment is not right for the first speaker to introduce the topic, it may never emerge at all.

Call–answer patterns in Asian discourse:

A: Call
B: Answer
A and B: 'Facework'
A: (topic)

The writers argue that this accounts for the sense of frustration often felt by Westerners in conversation with Asian speakers of English, or surprise when the topic appears to emerge only at the point when they are expecting the conversation to finish, or even a sense that conversation never reaches a satisfactory indication of topic at all.

This paper shows the strengths and weaknesses of the more subjective, non-quantitative approaches to language study. On the one hand, the insights are remarkably convincing and interesting. The fundamental point made is that as conversationalists we are governed by unconscious learned patterns of interaction and that it takes some effort to realise that they are not 'natural' or universal patterns. Secondly, the suggestion is that these unconscious patterns can reinforce cultural stereotypes when different patterns come together in the same conversation. Finally, the precise problem of the delayed topic introduction versus immediate topic introduction seems to fit many people's intuitive sense of what goes on in Asian–Western discourse. The paper therefore provides an elegant and intuitively satisfying explanation of the causes of a problem. On the other hand, the issue of how far one can generalise from particular instances, or what the exact scope of the terms used in the paper is, or how subjective the interpretation of the authors is, would all be the basis for potential criticisms of the paper.

In one sense, qualitative approaches lend themselves naturally to the domain of speech, since they acknowledge something of the complexity and ambiguity of actual interaction and the role of the researcher in the process of gaining greater understanding of a topic.

The cultural awareness which can be gained from broader, ethnographically oriented work on spoken discourse across languages can greatly enhance understanding of both student–teacher interaction and group dynamics in mixed nationality groups. While many of the significant religious, political and cultural differences which exist between students of different backgrounds are often well understood, the more subtle effects brought about by the expectations of conversational patterning need greater effort for their effects to be understood.

5.2.3 Theoretically oriented work on spoken discourse

The article which I am using as a basis for the discussion of how more theoretically oriented research on speech has been undertaken is Liberman (1998) 'When theories of speech meet the real world'. This is what is known as a 'position paper'. By this researchers mean that the research text in question (they are generally journal articles) encapsulates their stance on a broad topic and usually they deal with an issue which is somewhat contentious. These can be difficult to write as there is a need to both understand the ideas being criticised, summarise the relevant arguments and present a coherent alternative to them.

The idea under attack in Liberman (1998) is that the stream of speech is made up of individual segments of sound which are in turn decoded by the brain into comprehensible discourse. The whole article revolves around a single underlying question: why is it so much easier to learn to speak than it is to learn to write?

The more subtle point which Liberman is making is the following: if there really is a rough parity between arbitrary symbols which make up

---

Quote 5.4 Liberman's main research question

What did evolution do for speech that gave it such a biological advantage over writing/reading? A theory of speech – or more broadly, language – can avoid that question, as most do, but it cannot avoid implying an answer; and if that answer does not sit comfortably with the priority of speech, then the scientists should consider that they have got hold of the wrong theory.

(Liberman, 1998: 112)

writing systems and arbitrary sounds which make up speech why is speech not as cognitively challenging as writing?

Theoretical research questions very often begin life as 'what if . . . ?' thoughts, and in a 'position paper' these can, and are often intended to, present fundamental challenges to existing paradigms. It should be noted, however, that even the most theoretical thinkers are selective in what they present as 'given' and what is challenged. Liberman, for example, does not question his own fundamental assumption that speaking really *is* easier than writing. Nor does he address the issue of the extent and quality of the differences in the two learning processes. It could be argued, for instance, that it takes several years practising for ten or more hours a day for the child to become a fluent, grammatically standard (within the norms of their own social or family group) speaker.

Nonetheless, by framing a question which sums up his position so completely (the 'why is speaking easier than writing?' question), Liberman is able to develop a coherent line of thought which contrasts the inadequacies of conventional theory and generative phonology in the first half of the paper against the satisfactory nature of his less generally accepted stance presented in the second half (see Research summary).

Research summary: The structure of Liberman's discussion of his research question regarding the biological advantage of speech over writing and subsequent questions

Conventional theories of speech sounds suggest that they are not intrinsically any different from any other sounds in the world, but are the vehicles of meaningful segments of sound roughly equating to visual segments in a writing system.

$\downarrow$

This leads Liberman to his next question: if there is no biological basis for speech sounds 'how is it that people who cannot spell a single word – lacking even the awareness that words can be spelled – nevertheless find, each time they speak, that producing perfectly spelled phonetic structures is dead easy?'

$\downarrow$

Conventional theories also suggest that speech perception is a two-stage process in which the primary sounds are translated into phonetic elements by the brain. '. . . [T]he two processes are exactly parallel, requiring the same kind of cognitive step to endow their ordinary auditory and visual percepts with phonetic significance. Why, then, should the one be so much easier and more natural than the other?'

↓

Liberman at this point suggests that if ease of perception of discrete elements was the key to language, then the oral/aural channel was in fact *less* suitable than the visual/motoric.

↓

He then argues that by suggesting that language merely appropriated sounds to put them to the use of the language system, traditional theory has difficulty answering his initial question: what exactly was it that evolved?

It is remarkable how the flow of questions around which this first half of the paper is based dries up at the point when the writer begins to expand on his own theory. In the rest of the paper Liberman proposes a 'phonetic module' which deals directly with the sounds of speech and which requires no intervening processing or translation of these into any other form. These 'articulatory gestures of the vocal tract' are, he argues, the product of an evolutionary process rather than being standard sounds appropriated for the use of language. This work is interesting because it meets up with new ideas about the evolution of brain and language (for example Deacon, 1996) and also with recent work in neuro-linguistics.

Liberman's discussion shows the way a questioning technique can be used as the basis of both a critical evaluation of a theory, and a framework for presenting that evaluation. Secondly, by taking a step back from the data a theoretical approach can ask questions at a very universal or general level (some might argue too general and abstract). Finally, this kind of work can link up with more empirical approaches. For instance, there is an interesting parallel between Liberman's suggestions about the phonetic module and emerging work on mode in neuro-linguistics (see Section 5.3.3) which also suggest that there may be a-symmetries between spoken and written modes and how they are processed/accessed. Taken seriously by the language-teaching community such ideas might radically alter the approach and balance to teaching speech and writing.

5.3 Grammar, structural choices and the spoken language

5.3.1 A corpus informed approach

The paper discussed in detail in this section is one of several by the authors, growing from their work on 'CANCODE' (the Cambridge and

Nottingham Corpus of Discourse in English). This is an extensive collection of real speech data from a wide variety of genres and speakers. The paper argues that 'language teaching which aims to foster speaking skills and natural spoken interaction should be based upon the grammar of spoken language, and not on grammars which mainly reflect written norms' (Carter and McCarthy, 1995: 141). The material on which the insights about spoken grammar is based in this particular article is a 'mini-corpus' (taken from the larger spoken corpus) of selected conversational, narrative, 'service encounter' and 'language in action' genres. The selection is heavily weighted in favour of conversational data, however, since this is the core genre which the authors are interested in. The discussion is based on a very broad frequency analysis of the instances of the four features being discussed:

- ellipsis,
- left dislocation and topical information,
- reinforcement: the tail slot,
- indirect speech.

The method for each of these features is to introduce/explain them, to give several examples with a commentary and finally to relate them to previous work on pedagogic grammar. It is this linking up with teaching reference grammars, and the highlighting of the relevance for the classroom, rather than attempting to take on theoretical or computational grammars, which makes the work especially relevant and interesting for the teacher.

For example, rather than dealing with the issue of the precise definition of 'the grammar of spoken language' the authors simply take the four grammatical features with notable frequency in their samples and discuss these in relation to the work of Michael Swan or Louis Alexander, names which will be familiar to many teachers of English language. Furthermore, in later work (for instance Carter and McCarthy, 1997, or Carter, Hughes and McCarthy, 2000) the authors create more classroom-oriented and self-study material using and introducing some of the insights from earlier work, again with a particular emphasis on the distinctive features of spoken grammar. Therefore, these authors are an unusual example of academic researchers crossing the boundary between investigations into speech data and applications in the teaching context.

A potential criticism of the approach is the fact that after the initial description of the 'mini-corpus' and its weighting for conversational data there is reliance on expressions such as 'situational ellipsis is particularly apparent in casual data' or 'also recurrent in the mini-corpus are . . .'. Some readers, particularly those with a statistical bent, might require more precise quantitative statements before they were convinced of the need to include the features described in their core grammatical description. However, this issue simply returns us to the question raised earlier of how we judge what should be included in our spoken grammar, how far a grammar of speech overlaps with a more general grammatical model and how far a grammar for teaching a language is the same as a descriptive grammar of the language.

Next time you read an article on grammar, or indeed read a reference grammar, you might like to ask yourself how far spoken mode is taken into account. Also ask on what basis conclusions are reached. Are they on the basis of data or of intuition? What kind of data are used? What is the nature of the genre, register and style of the language examples used? Are the examples ones which you would find useful to teach your students?

Summary of methods/approach, Carter and McCarthy (1995)

Extended sets of examples to illustrate broad quantitative findings (rather than full statistical analysis) in relation to four grammatical features seen to be particularly interesting or salient. Features chosen for description are those particularly under-represented in previous descriptions of grammar. Frequencies and examples are taken from a 'mini-corpus' of speech data weighted towards conversational genres.

Further ideas about the role and status of grammar in relation to speech can be found in Leech (2000) (who here takes issue with the concept of 'a grammar of speech'), Glisan and Drescher (1993), who discuss the relationship between native speakers' grammar and grammars found in textbooks, or Call and Sotillo (1995), who suggest that, in the case of learning Spanish, students can gain a better grasp of tense by means of focused conversations with native speakers.

5.3.2 Speaking/writing variability

The second paper I use as an example of work dealing with structural choices in the context of speech is Haynes (1992) 'The development of speaking/writing variability in narratives of non-native English speakers'. This article takes some of the most central research findings about the variation in the grammatical and lexical 'texture' of spoken and written English (Biber, 1986; Biber 1988), and applies the findings in the context of second language learners. Whereas Carter and McCarthy (1995) bridges the gap between traditional pedagogic grammars and insights from real speech data, the present paper links an investigation about inter-language variability to previous work on how grammatical features cluster together across different modes to create a variety of spoken and written 'dimensions' or registers.

The paper is also another excellent example of a classically set up experimental, quantitative approach to the investigation of a research question, and of the strengths and weaknesses of this paradigm. The strengths are that issues of generalisability and objectivity are largely dealt with within the research model itself by researchers following traditional experimental methods. That is to say constructs such as 'control', 'variable', 'subject', together with the application of previous research methods to present data, all point to the researcher as having accepted these fundamentals of the classical quantitatively oriented approach as the best way forward with their research questions. Given the dominance of this stance across many academic disciplines the use of the quantitative framework and its building blocks helps the writer in the process of persuading the reader of the interest and substance of their findings.

Haynes is scrupulous in her outlining of the methods she used, and presents these in a very accessible way, despite the complexity of some of the quantitative methods. She also avoids the extreme impersonality of presentation which can mark out quantitative academic texts.

Thus Haynes scores highly on two aspects of the research process: overall transparency of communication and replicability of methods. Many academics seem keen to hide behind the complex presentation of their methods and/or write as if all their readers are familiar with the minutiae of their approach. In a 'hard' science discipline it is possible to use a short-hand presentation of methodology if standard procedures are being carried out. However, since in the applied sciences, and particularly applied linguistics there are few standardly accepted methods for dealing with data, and particularly speech data (for example, how far are speaker repetitions taken into account in the analysis or how much contextual information is noted?), it is crucial for the quantitative researcher to be capable of transparent communication.

Secondly, the presentation of methods should be not only clear but full and detailed enough for another researcher to undertake exactly the same study, should they want to verify the results for themselves. In fact, the clear and full presentation of a methodology and the individual methods which underpin it lend strength and persuasive power to a research report. If the researcher is seen to be confident enough to show all the workings which led them to their results and conclusion, this can be an indication that they are not skimming over any uncomfortable details and are happy for another researcher to check on their findings.

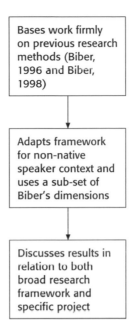

Figure 5.1   **Summary of research framework, Haynes (1992)**

Summary of methods/approach, Haynes (1992)

In the application of a selection of methods and findings from earlier work on variability between speech and writing in first language contexts (Biber, 1996 and Biber, 1988) to second language learners' inter-language in the two forms, a 'controlled' experimental approach was used:

'In this study I control for discourse contexts by investigating only spoken and written narratives. I control for other contextual factors by eliciting data in the same way from students of similar ages in the same environment. Additionally, I control for target language variability by comparing the spoken and written narratives of native speakers to those of non-native speakers' (Haynes, 1992: 45).

The narrative data (stories of the most frightening experience ever had by the subject) were taken from four groups: native speakers, and beginning, intermediate and advanced learners. These were then analysed for the patterns of co-occurrence of particular grammatical features and the findings related to previous work.

Haynes discovered that learners moved towards native speaker-like variability in a systematic way as they progressed from beginner to advanced levels.

Work which argues that there are in fact differences between variability in first and second language contexts can be found in Zuengler (1987) or Zobl (1984) 'The wave model of linguistic change and the naturalness of interlanguage'.

5.3.3   Grammar, brain function and modality

> **Quote 5.5**   Liberman on the biological basis of speech
>
> Speech, on the one side, is a product of biological evolution, standing as the most obvious, and arguably the most important, of our species-typical behaviors. Reading/writing, on the other, did not evolve biologically, but rather developed (in some cultures) as a secondary response to that which evolution had already produced. A consequence is that we are biologically destined to speak, not to read or write. Accordingly, we are all good at speech, but disabled as readers and writers.
>
> (Liberman, 1997: 4–5)

The final case study about the structure of language and the spoken form is from quite a different area from the first two, and uses a different research strategy. A growing area of interest in research into language and speech is the biological basis of the language faculty (see for instance the Liberman, 1997, quotation above). Related to this is the question of how the structure of the human brain is set up to deal with language, and, in general, how language is processed. In researching speech we are particularly interested in whether speech is organised and processed differently from writing.

This case study is in the field of neuro-linguistics and investigates the status of speech data in a brain-damaged patient who had distinctively different impairment in spoken and written forms (Rapp and Caramazza, 1997, 'The modality-specific organisation of grammatical categories: evidence from impaired spoken and written sentence production'). This begins with an extensive and useful review of previous work on modality in language-impaired subjects. In doing this the authors both point to the importance and interest of the work they are going to report, and highlight the need for the particular investigation. They then note the performance of the subject under investigation in a number of different tests of language and memory, and explain that the unusual patterning of impairment led them to want to investigate the question of mode more deeply.

They investigated the subject's sentence production in two ways: an analysis to quantify their initial impression that there were different proportions of nouns and function words in the two modes; and an analysis of the levels of accuracy or quality of the production in the two forms.

After testing and analysing the results in both these ways, they found confirmation of their impression that the errors were complementary in the two different modes. In spoken output there was a marked loss of all but grammatical or function words, whereas the written output was mainly made up of nouns. The implication of this is that all the linguistic information is still in the brain of the subject, but can only be accessed partially by either mode. Furthermore, there would appear to be significant regularity in what can/cannot be accessed by the spoken mode.

> **Quote 5.6** The starting point for Rapp and Caramazza's investigation
>
> Although [the subject's] written production of single words was markedly superior to his spoken production in object naming, the differences between his written and spoken descriptions of simple scenes could not be characterized as easily. For example, in describing a picture of a rock falling on a car [he] wrote: *car accident rock*. In contrast, in orally describing a picture of a truck crashing into a bus, he said: 'The /rʌz/ was a /kəzolnd/ at the /drʌʃ/ and he /kraezd/ into his /kard/ and /aez/ /mardʒ/ at the /sard/, at his /kard/, his /kard/.' The impression created by his speech was that it contained the syntactic elements as well as the prosody of appropriate sentences (albeit with very few recognizable content words), while his writing contained content words but lacked sentence structure. Thus, while his spoken output provided the surface features of seemingly intact syntactic processing and function word vocabulary, his written production exhibited difficulties with just these aspects of sentence production.
>
> (Rapp and Caramazza, 1997: 260)

Having discussed their results briefly the authors move on to a new research question: what are the characteristics of the underlying functional architecture in the brain which could show effects like these after damage? Given the theories of sentence processing on which they base their work, the authors are interested in how and why this subject can disassociate function and content words in this way in relation to speech and writing. To pursue the argument they posit three potential explanations of the fact that he can only produce mainly grammatical/function words in speech:

(a) specific sparing (and damage elsewhere) of bits of the brain to do with phonological encoding of these forms;

(b) there are far more function words, and their extreme familiarity protects them more strongly against damage;

(c) function words are generally shorter than nouns (and therefore easier to produce).

In terms of the last point, their method was to carry out further statistical analysis to show that differences between noun and function word production were seen at every word length, and therefore this factor could not be the explanation.

Having raised the issue of the frequency of grammatical/function words as against open-class words, they note that they could not investigate this more fully since the frequency range of the two sets had no overlap. The authors conclude that the differences in production must either be a result of the actual grammatical category and/or frequency differences.

The paper concludes with a lengthy discussion of the implications of the results, again following the pattern of a number of potential explanations or hypotheses dealt with in turn and either eliminated through close argument or set aside for further investigation due to a lack of conclusive evidence. They conclude that grammatical categories may be a salient feature of the representation, organisation and processing of independent, modality specific lexicons and that access to phonological and orthographic forms can occur independently. That is to say, the grammatical form of an item which a language user is attempting to produce may affect its processing in a way that is sensitive to whether delivery is via speech or writing.

This is a very tightly argued paper which uses hypotheses, questions and statistics in an interesting way to present a seamless 'narrative' of the research process. A schematic representation of the way the research process is presented to the reader is represented in Figure 5.2.

This structuring gives an appearance of a progression of the work which is both clear and logical, and the investigation backs up initial impressions by giving them a statistical basis. However, whereas many academics would be happy simply to have the statistical investigation as the main source of weight and persuasion in the paper (and write a paper both easier to read and half the length!), the authors use the statistical evidence largely to confirm their initial interpretation of the subject's language behaviour, before embarking on a very full theoretical discussion based on possible interpretations of the data. The paper, therefore, differs in its epistemological 'culture' from the majority of those in applied linguistics in that it does not assume that the noting of insights about language, and the subsequent support of these by statistical analysis is an acceptable concluding point for a paper.

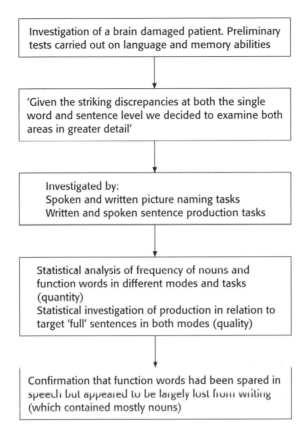

Figure 5.2   Summary of Rapp and Caramazza (1997)

Summary of methods/approach, Rapp and Caramazza (1997)

Statistical analyses of language output from a single subject is given in a variety of experimental contexts. Statistical data are used as confirmation of initial impression and a starting point for lengthy discussion of potential explanations for the findings. The strategy used in the discussions is that of setting up several alternative hypotheses which cover all the possible explanations for the results (at one point, for instance, they say 'we will mention [a possible explanation/cause] at least for the sake of completeness') to eliminate through argument all but the one they want to propose.

5.4   Research into fluency and pronunciation

There are three broad areas of research into pronunciation. The first looks at the influence of first language on the production in the target language. These are known as cross-linguistic approaches. Insights gained from research in this area can inform the teaching of particular monolingual groups and also aid the individual learner in understanding the special difficulties which the target language holds for them, due to the differences in the sound structure between it and their first language.

A second, more theoretically oriented, approach embeds research on fluency/pronunciation in the wider second language acquisition framework. This work can be either in a single language context, for example Towell, Hawkins and Bazergui (1996) ('The development of fluency in advanced learners of French'), or provide cross-linguistic comparison, for example Berg and Hassan (1996) ('The unfolding of suprasegmental representations: a cross-linguistic perspective'). Such work tends to remain at the more theoretical end of the teaching spectrum, rather than providing immediately applicable insights for the classroom.

Research summary

Towell *et al.* (1996) investigated the fluency of advanced learners of French. Based on the evidence of an increase in length and complexity of utterances after a period residing abroad they suggest that language learning in an immersion situation increases 'the degree of proceduralisation of knowledge' and that such learners have gained quicker access to syntactic and discourse knowledge for 'on-line speech production'.

A third general thread of research begins from more pragmatically or classroom-oriented questions, and frequently involves an experimental approach to answering them.

Research summary: Griffiths (1990): 'Speech rate and NNS comprehension: A preliminary study in time–benefit analysis'

'In L2 teaching, speaking at slower rates necessarily involves either saying less or increasing teacher-talk time: it would, therefore, be useful if teachers knew the rates at which listening comprehension is maximized to make the best use of that scarce resource, time' (Griffiths, 1990: 312)

Griffiths investigates this issue via a straightforward experiment in which non-native speakers listened to passages read at three different speeds. While moderately fast reading (200 words per minute) significantly reduced comprehension, there was not a significant difference between average (150 wpm) and slow (100 wpm) rates in terms of comprehension.

More interesting, perhaps, in the context of work on fluency is Griffiths' finding that listeners' perceptions of speech rates are not reliable. 'As the NNSs [non-native speakers] in this study appear only marginally capable of detecting SR [speech rate] differences and the NSs [native-speakers] appear to be inconsistent in doing so, the issue of SR awareness must be seen as requiring further investigation' (Griffiths, 1990: 331–332). Griffiths relates this back to the issue of teacher-talk speed; however, for the student interested in researching pronunciation and fluency these findings (which confirm earlier work) suggest a very interesting research question in relation to learner production: what factors affect listeners' perceptions of fluency and speed of delivery?

5.4.1   An inter-lingual study

> **Quote 5.7** Osborne's research aims in 'Final cluster reduction in English L2 speech: A case study of a Vietnamese speaker'
>
> In attempting to determine the relative role of native language influence in learners' second language phonology, few areas have received as much attention as interlanguage syllable structure. And in explaining how learners render unfamiliar second language syllables pronounceable, few proposed rules have been as prominent as cluster reduction, formalized by Eckman (1986). Theories of second language phonology based on traditional ideas of contrast, of interlanguage development, of markedness differentials, and of parameter setting all rely on the concepts of a rule of cluster reduction to make their analyses work. This paper examines one aspect of second language syllable structure, syllable-final clusters, in the English of a Vietnamese L1 speakers. Extending Benson's (1988) analysis, it shows how errors apparently not due to native language influence can be so attributed using the cluster reduction rule. Furthermore, it shows that the position of a reduced consonant can be largely predicted based on interaction with other rules, universal considerations, and native language syllable structure.
>
> (Osborne, 1996: 164)

Osborne (1996) investigates the aspect of pronunciation known as 'clusters'. A cluster is a group of two or more consonant sounds next to one another in a syllable. In English, for example, the word 'facts' ends with a cluster of three consonant sounds together: /k/, /t/, /s/. Different languages permit different combinations of consonant sounds to be pronounced together. Andrea Osborne's paper contains an intensive analysis of one aspect of these features, final cluster reduction. 'Final clusters' are those at the end of words and 'cluster reduction' is when one or more of the consonants are missing.

Osborne uses this investigation to address the bigger issues of:

• how far variability in this feature is predictable,
• how far any predictability can be accounted for by the influence of the speaker's first language,
• the particular influence of the structure of final syllables in the mother-tongue.

She presents a statistical analysis of the final clusters produced by the subject in question, a Vietnamese advanced user of English, during two taped business meetings taken six years apart (1985 and 1991).

Osborne concludes that whereas previous work has suggested that final cluster reduction was largely unpredictable in non-native speakers, unlike the reduction which happens in fast speech of native speakers, there was in fact a clear pattern to the dropping of consonants in the subject in question. Furthermore, she argues that the influence of the first language syllable structure can be seen at work.

Osborne's paper raises several issues which are of general interest in teaching and researching pronunciation and fluency: the status of the model for pronunciation studies, the interrelationship between pronunciation and grammar, and the influence of methodology on the type of findings available.

Native speakers, when they are speaking naturally and quickly, carry out consonant reduction or elimination. For example, in the word 'football' the /t/ sound is very generally not present. Research into syllable structure suggests that this is a regular, predicable process in native speakers, but highly variable in non-native speakers. Osborne questions this, as outlined above, but the more general issue, and one of particular interest, is where the model for the underlying syllable structure comes from in the first place. Given the fact that of all aspects of research into language phonology is based firmly on the spoken mode, it is notable that the unmarked or base version of syllable structure is strongly influenced by the written form. To take the case of 'football' it is assumed that the full, underlying form of the first syllable is /fʊt/ despite the fact that the default for natural speech is /fʊb/ or more likely /fʊp/.

A second area of interest in relation to work on pronunciation relates to the interface between inter-language grammar and language production. Osborne notes a particular difficulty in the study of cluster reduction which is how to decide whether the leaving off of a morphologically significant sound is a production error or reveals a lack of grammatical knowledge. For instance, the sound /s/ forms the second person singular ending of present tense verbs in English: 'Tessa likes fishing'. If a learner

Table 5.1   **Methods and findings**

Research Project 1 Method A	Research Project 2 Method A (with refinements)	Research Project 3 Method B (unrelated method)
Conclusion: Little or no evidence that L2 syllable production is influenced by L1 syllable structure.	Conclusion: Evidence that L2 syllable production *is* to an extent influenced by L1 syllable structure.	Conclusion: Evidence that L2 syllable structure *is* to an extent influenced by L1 structure

Note: The findings of project 2, being based largely on the same methods as 1, may in fact make a stronger case. Where there are big methodological differences these should not be used as the main explanation of differences between results.

produces the verb without the /s/ sound, 'Tessa like fishing', the question is whether this is a case of final cluster reduction (i.e. the learner knows that the verb takes the /s/ ending but avoids using the sound because of pronunciation difficulties) or a grammatical error. These issues become particularly clear when natural speech as opposed to elicited data is used.

In relation to the latter, Osborne points out that many previous studies on the topic are based on unnatural speaking tasks, rather than spontaneous speech. She uses this in her conclusion to explain partially the differences between her findings and earlier work. However, the bigger issue for those interested in research methods generally is the level of acceptability of comparing data compiled under such different conditions. If data are gathered by very different means from earlier studies with which a comparison is being made there is a danger of circularity in the conclusion. A hypothetical set of studies is shown in Table 5.1 to illustrate this.

5.4.2   A quantitative approach to investigating fluency

Lennon (1990) 'Investigating fluency in EFL: A quantitative approach' is interesting because it turns on its head one of the assumptions about fluency and looks at the topic from a different angle from most researchers. While many pronunciation studies focus on the language learner and the speech they produce, Lennon's central research question is 'What do listeners perceive as fluent or non-fluent speech?'. His more specific questions could be phrased as:

- What linguistic features function as indicators of perceived fluency?
- Can we quantify these linguistic features?
- Can we develop an objective test for fluency?

> **Quote 5.8** Lennon's research aims in: 'Investigating fluency in EFL:
> A quantitative approach'
>
> This paper investigates various easily quantifiable performance features that might function as objective indicators of oral fluency. It would be advantageous if we could assemble a set of variables that functioned as good indicators of what expert judges, such as experienced native speaker EFL teachers, are reacting to when subjectively assessing fluency. This would advance our knowledge of what constitutes fluency and especially what makes for perceived fluency differences among learners and how an individual learner improves in fluency over time.
>
> (Lennon, 1990: 387)

> **Quote 5.9** Lennon on two senses of fluency
>
> **The broad sense**
> In the 'broad' sense fluency appears to function as a cover term for oral proficiency. In this sense, fluency represents the highest point on a scale that measures spoken command of a foreign language. . . . This broad sense also carries over into common parlance, where to be fluent in a foreign language is a mark of social accomplishment. . . .
>
> **The narrow sense**
> In its narrower sense, fluency in EFL refers to one, presumably isolatable, component of oral proficiency. This sense is found particularly in procedures for grading oral examinations, and many readers will be familiar with having to score candidates for fluency as well as, perhaps, correctness, idiomaticness, relevance, appropriateness, pronunciation, lexical range, and so on.
>
> (Lennon, 1990: 389)

Lennon suggests that 'fluency is an impression on the listener's part' and goes on to present an investigation of what makes up that impression. In order to do this he tested four German native speaker subjects with similar levels of English close to the start of a period of study in Britain and again at the end, five months later. Their task was to re-tell a story from a set of pictures. These stories were recorded and played to a panel of nine native speakers of English who were asked to score the subjects' fluency. Without knowing whether the versions were the earlier or the later rendition the panel members agreed which of each pair of stories seemed the more fluent, and in each case this tallied with the later narrative.

Lennon then went on to try to uncover what possible linguistic signals led to this judgement. In order to do this he categorised 12 fluency factors which embraced both the broader and the narrower senses of fluency, and produced comparative statistics for each subject and each story, earlier and later.

Concept 5.2   **Quantifiable factors in fluency (based on Lennon, 1990)**

Words per minute (including repetitions)

Words per minute (excluding repetitions)

Repetitions

Self-corrections

Filled pauses

Repetitions and self-corrections as a percentage of total speech

Unfilled pause time as percentage of total speech time

Filled pause time as percentage of total speech time

Mean length of speech 'runs' between pauses, in words

Percentage of T-Units followed by pause

Percentage of total pause time at all T Unit boundaries

Mean pause time at T-Unit boundaries

Note: Unless otherwise stated these are counted per T-Unit

Lennon found that the later storytelling attempt was, perhaps unsurprisingly, lower in pauses and higher in terms of words per minute in the case of all four subjects at the end of their period of study in Britain. The subjects also tended to have longer 'runs' of speech between pauses, but showed similar levels of self-correction to their original attempts at the narrative. One subject had a different profile of dysfluency features from the rest, and this led Lennon to suggest that there might be two distinct aspects to fluency which he termed 'the temporal component' (for example, speed of delivery or percentage of pause time) and the 'vocal dysfluency marker component' (for example, repetitions or filled-pauses). Three of the subjects had actually increased their self-correction and yet this did not affect the native speakers' judgements of the levels of fluency. This suggested to Lennon that self-correction may even be one of the features which lead listeners to perceive native speaker-like fluency in the task of speech delivery.

The main features which seemed to affect judgements of fluency according to Lennon's findings are:

- words per minute (excluding repetitions),
- filled pauses,
- percentage of T-Units followed by a pause.

Note, however, that the author does not raise the issue in his discussion or his background to the study about how universal these measures of fluency might be. For example, in certain cultures, notably Japanese, there is a higher tolerance of silence in conversational exchanges. Therefore, the judgements of this panel will be culturally constrained by their own perceptions of what it is to be fluent.

Three of Lennon's measures related to the positioning of pauses and he suggests that 'mispositioning' of pauses (i.e. placing them within T-Units rather than at the end where they would naturally be placed) strongly influences impressions of fluency.

Further work looking at the issue of what exactly makes a learner sound fluent or un-fluent can be found in Browning (1985).

5.4.3   A distributional approach to how we understand speech

> **Quote 5.10** Saffran, Newport and Asin's research aims in: 'Word segmentation: The role of distributional cues'
>
> One of the infant's first tasks in language acquisition is to discover the words embedded in a mostly continuous speech stream. This learning problem might be solved by using distributional cues to word boundaries – for example, by computing the transitional probabilities between sounds in the language input and using the relative strengths of these probabilities to hypothesize word boundaries. The learner might be further aided by language-specific prosodic cues correlated with word boundaries. As a first step in testing these hypotheses, we briefly exposed adults to an artificial language in which the only cues available for word segmentation were the transitional probabilities between syllables. Subjects were able to learn the words of this language. Furthermore, the addition of certain prosodic cues served to enhance performance. These results suggest that distributional cues may play an important role in the initial word segmentation of language learners.
>
> (Saffran, Newport and Asin, 1996: 606)

One of the major questions in language acquisition is the extent of the role in learning a language of an inherent language faculty as opposed to external linguistic influences. This paper addresses the significant theoretical question via an investigation of how a child learns to distinguish word boundaries in the spoken form of their mother tongue. Saffran, Newport and Asin (1996) argue that since the stream of speech is continuous (there is no equivalent in the spoken form to the spaces before and after words in writing), and the sounds which make up meaningful words in different languages are so widely varied, it is not feasible to suggest universal rules underlying the acquisition of word boundary knowledge. Rather these researchers suggest that word boundary discrimination is a complex, distributionally governed learning task (as opposed to automatic acquisition process) based on a child's perceptions of the relative distribution of sounds in the language. These relations they call 'distributional cues'. How do you investigate this suggestion in infants who can barely speak?

Concept 5.3   **What is a word?**

It is difficult to step back from one's own language and realise that we rarely utter words in clear isolation from one another. Rather, spoken words are embedded in the stream of speech in such a way that when we listen to an unfamiliar language it is difficult to begin to distinguish where one word begins and another ends. What shared features, then do all spoken words have which may help the child (or the language learner) distinguish one from another?

- A word is a sequence of sounds (or 'phones') which can be moved around in a sentence: /buks/ are kept in libraries – librarians look after /buks/.

- A word is generally uttered as a whole and pauses or other items do not come in the middle of it (some languages break this rule by putting grammatically important information in the middle of words by a process called 'infixation').

- A word is a series of sounds in a fixed order. If you change this order you get either a different word or a non-word: pat – tap. (based on Saffran, Newport and Asin, 1996: 608)

Researchers into child language acquisition are intrigued by the question of how a child learns to distinguish one word from another. Earlier work suggested that the child may use the higher and lower frequencies of particular sound combinations to distinguish word boundaries, with the suggestion that where a series of phones shows a wide range of possible following phones the potential for a word boundary exists, and where there is a limited number of following phones it is not.

Saffran, Newport and Asin (1996) aimed to formalise earlier subjective work on the topic by means of a statistical analysis called 'transitional probability'.

Concept 5.4   **Transitional probability**

This statistical technique is based on the patterns of co-occurrence of items. The probability of the sequence of two items following one another is calculated on the basis of the frequency of the pair in order divided by the frequency of the first item:

$$\frac{\text{Frequency of pair XY}}{\text{frequency of X}}$$

Where there is a high transitional probability the presence of X strongly suggests Y will follow. The lower the transitional probability score, the less likely the pair XY.

In terms of distinguishing word boundaries, within word syllable-pairs, they can be analysed in this way. Saffran, Newport and Asin (1996: 610) use the following pair of sample equations comparing the sequence of sounds in the word 'baby' and the non-word 'baytoo'; the first, they suggest will have a higher transitional probability score than the second:

$$\frac{\text{Frequency of bay.bi}}{\text{frequency of bay}}$$

$$\frac{\text{Frequency of bay\#too}}{\text{frequency of bay}}$$

Transitional frequency calculation differs from scoring the probability of a straightforward co-occurrence of pairs of sounds. The latter process would suggest that very common pairs of sounds such as *article + noun* in English (for example, a + boy) could be candidates for taking on the status of words.

Transitional frequency, in contrast, takes special account of the frequency of the first syllable in the language as a whole. In the case of a first syllable being very frequent, such as an article, this shows that the relative probability of the co-occurrence of a pattern such as a + boy is actually quite low.

Saffran, Newport and Asin (1996) created a nonsense language made up of English syllables to carry out an experiment designed to investigate how language learners might use transitional frequency clues to distinguish word boundaries. Within this language six 'words' (i.e. stable combinations of the same syllables in the same order) were created and played to subjects in a carefully designed stream of similar but non-word syllable combinations (i.e. unstable random sequences) from the 'language'. Their results showed that subjects scored significantly better than would have been predicted by chance when asked to say what were potential candidates for words from the language after listening to three seven-minute blocks of the nonsense language. Furthermore subjects found it easier to learn words with higher transitional probability scores than those with lower.

The researchers note that distributional cues are probably not the only mechanism by which word segmentation is learned (prosodic and rhythmic cues probably play a part as well), and that there is little evidence of whether humans actually use statistical mechanisms to learn the words of a language.

This kind of work is of particular interest since, as Saffran, Newport and Asin (1996) tentatively observe, a strong statement of its implications would suggest that language can be learned via an innate capacity for 'distributional learning' rather than innate knowledge of language. In the context of research into speech and its status in the enterprise of theoretical and applied linguistic research more generally, the work is particularly noteworthy as it is founded on sound-based units (as opposed to constructs dependent on the written form) – the syllable. Furthermore, it carries out the analysis of syllable relations in the context of human memory and learning abilities and by so doing raises important questions about wider theoretical issues in the language learning/acquisition debate.

5.5 Summary

This chapter has presented a variety of case-studies exemplifying different approaches to linguistic enquiry at various 'levels' in our conceptualisation of speech. Throughout the discussions the central questions have been how the researchers' work relates to bigger, more generalisable, ideas of spoken mode, how far mode has *really* been considered seriously by the projects, and what insights the studies give us into the place of spoken discourse in 'language' or 'applied linguistics'.

Further reading

Biber, D. (1988). *Variation across Speech and Writing*. Cambridge: Cambridge University Press. (Provides a particularly useful appendix of examples of features used in the analysis, and links these to background reading.)

Biber, D., Johansson, S., Leech, G., Conrad, S. and Finegan, E. (1999). *Longman Grammar of Spoken and Written English*. Harlow: Longman. (An extensive descriptive grammar based on corpus results.)

Carter, R. and McCarthy, M. (1995). Grammar and the spoken language. *Applied Linguistics*, 16/2: 141–158. (A useful and thought-provoking introduction to some of the main ideas about spoken grammar.)

Carter, R. and McCarthy, M. (forthcoming). *The Cambridge Advanced Grammar of English*. Cambridge: Cambridge University Press. (An extensive reference grammar which combines corpus and discourse insights.)

Deacon, T. W. (1996). Prefrontal coretex and symbol learning: why a brain capable of language evolved only once, in Boris M. Velichkovsky and D. M. Rumbaugh (Eds), *Communicating Meaning: the evolution and development of language*. Mahwah, NJ: Lawrence Erlbaum Associates. (An accessible outline of an innovative approach to thinking about language, with particular relevance to the spoken form.)

Kasper, G. and Blum-Kulka, S. (1993). *Interlanguage Pragmatics*. New York: Oxford University Press. (Standard text which summarises many of the issues in the inter-language argument.)

Chapter 6

Some new directions

This chapter will ...

- provide a reminder of some of the key theoretical issues in researching speech;
- review some of the significant developments in research into language processing;
- relate findings on speech, memory and language processing to the broader language teaching context.

6.1 Introduction

This chapter provides a brief conclusion to Section II, drawing together and summarising the theoretical issues of Section I, and the more applied research described in this section in order to provide a background to the suggestions for research into speaking which are given in Section III. In particular, this chapter introduces a selection of research into speech which is being carried out in related disciplines, for example neuro-linguistics or psychology. This chapter suggests ways in which this material can be relevant starting points for original work on speech in applied linguistics and language teaching.

To start to bring together the theory and the practice, let me first revise my stance taken in the earlier chapters, and in particular the point I made about the lack of attention to spoken mode in its own terms in the field.

Summary box: Mode in first and second language acquisition

In first language acquisition studies, 'speech', as the sole mode for first language acquisition, can for all practical purposes, be regarded as synonymous with 'language'.

Child language acquisition study therefore has no need to deal with the question of mode.

From this follows the fact that first language acquisition study has no need for a unified theory of 'speech' as opposed to 'language'.

When the a-modal first language acquisition paradigm is transferred to second language contexts there is still very little attention paid to the 'speech' versus 'language' issue.

However, language learning taking place in the framework of explicit pedagogy may need to distinguish mode more effectively than learning taking place via a first language single mode.

This is particularly the case as by contrast the written form is the focus of a great deal of explicit pedagogy in both first and second language contexts.

6.2   Mode-based research

Quote 6.1   McDonough and Shaw on the status of speech

As a language skill, speaking is sometimes undervalued or, in some circles, taken for granted. There is a popular impression that writing, particularly literature, is meant to be read and as such is prestigious, whereas speaking is often thought of as 'colloquial', which helps to account for its lower priority in some teaching contexts.

(McDonough and Shaw, 1993: 151)

The status of speech in applied linguistics is a little problematic as the previous chapters and the discussion above suggest. Much of the theory underpinning language teaching is a-modal, yet in other academic disciplines there is growing evidence that language is organised and processed quite differently according to mode. While the previous chapters discussed some of the issues surrounding a-modal views of language, this chapter looks more closely at the relationships between spoken and written forms to tease out some of the peculiarities of speech. The following sections outline some of the recent work on mode and use it as starting points for possible research of relevance to the classroom.

6.3 Theoretical orientations on the role and status of speech

In terms of language theory, the speech–writing binary is being addressed by scholars at levels of cognitive modelling, processing and memory constraints, as well as biology/neuro-physiology. Fundamental to many of these is the assumption that the ways these two forms are produced and perceived significantly affect the nature of the two, attitudes to them, and how they relate to our conceptualisation of language – an argument I pursue elsewhere in more detail (Hughes, 1996, especially Chapter 5).

6.3.1   The influence of the written form on our view of speech

The first thread is most consistently argued by David Olson who has long been interested in the cognitive impact of writing, and in *The World on Paper* (Olson, 1996b) argues that writing not only 'provides a conceptual model for' speech, but also that the very existence of that script-based model 'blind[s] us toward other features of language which are equally important to human communication but for which the script provides no adequate model' (Olson, 1996b). Over the years many others have argued, with varying degrees of plausibility and strength, for the impact of literacy on how we conceive of and use language. For example, Ong (1971) discusses the influence on language of technology; Jack Goody's work (most recently in Goody, 2000) provides an ethnographic analysis of the influence of the written word on society and thought (see also de Kerkehove, 1986; Harris, 1989).

For teachers and scholars interested in the skill of speaking the underlying question is 'what if our conceptual model of speech is defined and constrained by the existence of writing?'. While speaking would retain its primacy, the status and role of writing as a representational system would be altered. For as long as writing is a visual system dependent in the final analysis on the spoken we have very little need to worry about our learners' ability to become second language writers. We assume that, if they are literate in their first language, the written form will naturally follow the acquisition of the spoken. However, other recent work in diverse areas is challenging any unproblematic statement of the relationship between the two forms.

6.3.2   The influence on speech of memory and processing

Within a systemic paradigm Joachim Grabowski (1996) addresses the processing differences between the forms and argues that in approaching mode we should sift out 'process-related necessities' (for example, human memory constraints) from matters that are social and pragmatic (i.e. incidental features of the two forms, rather than defining ones).

Concept 6.1   **The systemic paradigm**

Systemic linguistics is based on a fundamental assumption that the function to which a stretch of language is put, and the context in which it occurs will affect the structural choices made by language users. The most influential figure in systemic (or functional) linguistics is M. A. K. Halliday. His approach to the description of language has been particularly widely used in pedagogic approaches to literacy and language study in Australia. Many of the cornerstones of systemic linguistics, for example the need to look beyond grammatical rules which hold within the sentence to explain language choices, are now becoming more widely accepted within the field of Applied Linguistics.

Within the realm of biology and neurology scholars are addressing questions relating to key assumptions about language, for example why speaking is easier than writing (Liberman, 1998) or why within the animal kingdom even very simple language systems have never evolved (Deacon, 1996).

Liberman controversially suggests that an explanation for the human pre-disposition for spoken language is that the fabric of speech takes the form of inherent phonetic 'gestures' evolved for that purpose by the speech organs, rather than the more general model of sounds put to use as the medium for spoken language. Since writing does not have the same evolutionary basis but must depend on a translation of these natural forms it is, Liberman argues, cognitively more challenging. Perhaps more compelling is Deacon's (1996) experimentally based work arguing that the human brain and the capacity for speech communication evolved hand-in-hand. In accounting for the evolutionary development of a massive prefrontal cortex in the human brain, Deacon sees evidence of the highly complex kind of learning needed for language, a type of learning which would, he argues, be highly inefficient in situations other than linguistic communication, and indeed carry a great cost to the organism in terms of learning effort (Deacon, 1996).

Deacon does not relate these conclusions to mode distinctions *per se*, but in the same field Eckart Scheerer argues that there is a fundamental cognitive dichotomy between speech and writing, that they represent 'two modes of cognitive functioning' (Scheerer, 1996: 227), that whereas writing is best defined as a symbolic system seen within historical and cultural developments the primary oral form should be regarded as a connectionist or sub-symbolic processing system.

What these views share is an acknowledgement of the importance and impact of the processing differences of the two forms, whether as with Olson at a high level where the script-based conception of language influences (and limits) our models of language, or at an explanatory level where the differing cognitive challenges of the two forms are posited as explaining some other fact (for instance the universal capacity for human speech over literacy).

6.3.3   Why are these ideas relevant to research into speech?

Taken together these theoretical stances provide intriguing starting points for language pedagogy. There has been a tendency in applied linguistic and linguistic theory for the assumption to be that (a) mode is largely irrelevant; (b) if mode is considered, then there is an implicit equation of the language faculty with the faculty of speech and links sought between syntax or the lexicon and phonological rules, conventionally the written form; (c) due to an implicit assumption of dependency of the written form on the spoken there is little impetus for any research into direct coding between syntax or the lexicon and the written; (d) most importantly, there has been little research into speaking as a faculty or topic in its own right within the field.

While there is little in the stances reviewed above to challenge the primacy of the spoken form (indeed there is much to cement it in position as an evolutionary faculty which developed hand in hand with the brain itself), there is a great deal to challenge any straightforward one-to-one relationship between spoken and written forms.

This in turn may lead us to wish to reassess the position of speech and writing in our theories, and the interrelations between writing and speech in second language acquisition studies, and in the curriculum. In particular, in the light of the notion that writing may not be as strongly dependent on the spoken as conventional wisdom has it, and that literacy affects our conceptualisation of language, there may be fruitful work on the precise role of writing in language learning and in relation to speed of acquisition of speaking skills.

The next section presents further evidence for the mode-specific view of language, this time from the point of view of work on speech pathology and memory.

6.4   Evidence from speech pathology

6.4.1   Brain, speech and writing

Several studies in speech pathology are providing further compelling evidence for the non-a-modal structuring of the human language faculty. Pound (1996) describes a brain-damaged patient whose written spelling performance was markedly worse than her oral spelling ability and concluded that speech and writing may not share the same output buffer in terms of language production. Croisilie *et al.* (1996) again suggest separation for the two processes (oral versus written spelling) via their work comparing Alzheimer's patients' abilities against a control group. In this case they account for the poorer results in *oral* spelling by Alzheimer's patients by suggesting that this process (spelling out words) has higher attentional demands than writing them. More recently Miceli and Capasso provide an excellent overview of past work on the topic of independence versus dependency of writing on speech, concluding that the bulk of the evidence with brain-damaged patients falls in favour of the independence of phonology and orthography. They posit a weak and a strong hypothesis as to the relationship between the two, the strong version suggesting 'phonological and orthographic word forms are not directly connected, but are allowed to interact via sublexical phonology–orthography and orthography–phonology conversion procedures' (Miceli and Capasso, 1997: 761), or, more simply, orthographic word forms come directly from semantics without an intervening phonological 'translation' process. Shelton and Weinrich (1997) present further evidence for a separation between the lexicons of the two forms via their work with an aphasic stroke patient and his differing abilities in producing spoken and written descriptions (see also the discussion of Rapp and Caramazza' work in Chapter 5).

These kinds of study suggest a clear distinction between the attentional demands of the two forms, the output and processing of them and the coding or representation of them in the brain.

6.4.2   Why does evidence of a 'modal' brain matter for future research on spoken mode?

There are implications for teaching which flow from these kinds of conclusion. I suggest three of the several which could be pursued: (a) if writing provides direct access to the semantic level without a necessary intervening phonological stage, the status of writing as input in language learning is, potentially, altered. That is to say, rather than being an adjunct to the learners' main task of learning to speak (i.e. learning the language, and it is argued elsewhere that the conflation of speech and language may not be helpful) writing could become a source of language learning impetus in its own right; (b) the notion that in the aural/oral channel syntactic patterning can exist as a skeletal framework of rhythm, intonation and function words presents a strong challenge to lexically based accounts of grammar, and such ideas may have practical application in teaching fluency or pronunciation linked to grammatical structures; (c) if spoken grammar and written grammar are coded differently in the brain we may wish to investigate these differences to enhance our teaching, or at a theoretical level pursue the point in language production at which mode 'kicks in'. In terms of the latter, recent work on language processing, memory and mode are perhaps particularly relevant, and I describe some of these in the next section.

6.5 Modality, processing and memory

6.5.1 Processing and handling speech versus writing

The focus of the majority of the papers described here is on speech or writing as an external modality and on the effects of differences between these on how we communicate and remember. Scholars in fields as diverse as psychoanalysis, autism studies, human–computer interaction, as well as psycholinguistics are seriously addressing the question of the role of mode in human understanding and communication. Clancier (1998) argues that whereas spoken narrative is the traditional vehicle for psychoanalytical dialogue the greater distancing effect of the written form may in fact be beneficial. Forsey, Kay-Raining-Bird and Bedrosian (1996) analysed interactions with adults with autism involving speech only or a combination of spoken and typed messages and concluded that the written mode could help with the production of longer utterances. Daly-Jones et al. (1997) concluded that messages involving a combination of the spoken and written in tandem were preferred by subjects and remembered better. De Gelder and Vroomen (1997) experimented with the recall of aural and visual, linguistic and non-linguistic information. From the patterns of recall they concluded that spoken input has a different status from both non-speech, writing and pictures. Tavassoli (1998) experimented with the presentation of information via different modes and concluded that recall was best via 'simultaneous bimodal presentation'.

6.5.2 Why do these processing issues matter in the classroom?

While these experiments largely deal with serial recall or isolated elements the notion that mode can affect memory and communicative efficacy has implications for the classroom. Once again I present examples of the kinds of thing which follow from such research: (a) for tasks where we would like students to improve recall, for example in a focus-on-form context, we may wish to pursue the notion that aural linguistic information has a particular relation to other aural input and that bimodal presentation may enhance ability to remember; (b) presentation via either mode may need to be reassessed in the light of the interrelations and processing demands of the two forms. For example, Forsey, Kay-Raining-Bird and Bedrosian (1996) suggested that processing demands were highest when subjects were required to write while being spoken to. In classroom contexts quite often tasks require students to do this, for example, interactive group work involving fact finding and note making, or even additional spoken information from the teacher about a writing task intended to help a student carry out the task.

The following section deals with the issues of mode in teaching contexts in more detail, and in particular the interrelations between speech and the written form.

6.6 Speaking, writing and teaching spoken/ written forms of language

Melanie Sperling's (1996) review of the speech/writing dichotomy provides a clear statement of the issues involved in attitudes to them in a pedagogic context, and at levels of analysis above the phoneme/grapheme. I will be attempting to relate her insights to the language (particularly English language) teaching context, where possible, and also to the wider issues for the spoken mode raised in the rest of this chapter by challenging to the necessity of a direct relationship between speech and the written form of language.

In the case of the first, polarised, view of the two forms, the emphasis is on the transference or re-interpretation of skills – such as narrative, which children may develop naturally – from one mode to the other. Also highlighted in the assumptions of this oppositional conception of the forms is the tendency for researchers to see the spoken form as in some way competing with the written: 'Because individuals are adept at and familiar with using language orally, writing is a task often burdened by habits established in oral contexts, and learning to write means, in part, learning to shake such habits' (Sperling, 1996: 54). Thus a strong statement of the oppositional view has speech 'interfering' with writing, and a weaker one has speaking skills and genres needing to be re-taught to be made more appropriate in the alien channel.

In either case the 'unnatural' nature of writing when conceived in opposition to speech in this way implies that a different set of teaching skills would be appropriate for the two forms. The issue of naturally acquired speech and necessarily instructed writing, which underlies Sperling's argument in turn raises the question of the role of instruction in the process of language learning generally. And, although Sperling's discussion takes place in a non-EFL context, this question is a particularly pertinent one for foreign and second language contexts.

When the two forms are conceived of as fundamentally similar, however, and the written is regarded as a conversation carried out by other means (a metaphor which underpins much process-based writing instruction, conference-based writing tasks and so on) a different set of benefits and issues arise. The particular benefit of teaching writing as dialogue with a reader is that it moves the writing task in the classroom context away from a mechanical process of trying to 'please teacher' and can draw on individual student's social, communicative and cognitive knowledge which may in turn benefit students whose background does not enable them to take naturally to the academic culture. However, interactive writing instruction, whether conceived of as text-as-interaction or at a meta-level text as focus for spoken interaction with peers or teachers about the process of writing, brings costs as well as benefits. In particular, the time-consuming nature of the interactive approach to writing instruction, and the variability of process-writing classroom management are mentioned by Sperling as of concern.

In both cases, when speech is conceptualised in opposition to writing and when it is seen as essentially similar, Sperling implies a wealth of research opportunity based on the speech/writing framework. In the case of the oppositional view she suggests a need for further consideration of the relations between language use in the home domain versus the classroom.

Quote 6.2 Sperling on the influence of speech on writing

We still do not know...whether or how different social or cultural spoken strategies show up systematically in students' school writing, because we lack broad-based studies that examine ways of communicating in students' communities and families and relate these ways to the writing that students do in school. Perhaps most importantly, we do not yet know how spoken-language influences for students considered mainstream...compare with the influences other students are said to experience when they write.

(Sperling, 1996: 63)

6.6.1   Applying Sperling's dichotomies to the second language research context

The complexities of this matrix of influences – speech communities, literacy, literate appropriacy, and so on – are added to when we look at them from a second language perspective. Sperling hints at the emerging first language writer being strongly dependent on social influences which go far beyond an isolated linguistic faculty (echoing Scheerer's (1996) speech–writing dichotomy which sees the written form as fundamentally historically and culturally defined). How much greater then are the subtle and complex issues when inter-linguistic, inter-cultural and inter-literate points of comparison are made. To take just one example, Kinoshita (1998) argues that the role of phonology is less strong in the interpretation of Japanese text than English. If we accept this, then at a theoretical level we may wish to pursue questions of whether different scripts permit different levels of necessary phonological encoding, and how this affects second language learning (and, more particularly, reading).

In the case of the complementary view Sperling again suggests that there are wide opportunities for fruitful research.

Quote 6.3   Research opportunities arising from viewing speech and writing as importantly different from one another

Importantly for both pedagogy and theory, we...lack studies that attempt to understand the relationship between the writer in the process of speaking to others in conversational contexts and the writer in the actual process of writing. Behind the assumption that writing is conversational is an indication that speaking and writing are dialogically the same; however, it is clear that the two situations are usually different.... Research working within a conversational framework that accounts for the ways writers make such choices is critical if the conversational model is to be fully useful in instruction.

(Sperling, 1996: 73)

She concludes that this style of research which begins at the 'intersection' of writing and conversation will throw us back on the significance of the differences between the two forms.

Sperling's summary of the issues, and her conclusion that mode interrelationships have significance educationally are echoed in work on developmental and educational psychology. For example, Mason (1998) investigated the role of oral and written discourse in the science classroom in a process of 'talking-to-learn', and concluded that subsequent writing showed evidence of changes to concept formation on the basis of oral discussion. Jones' (1998) work with oral (computer generated) feedback on writing suggested that linguistic complexity in writing strongly correlated with the use of such feedback, and Reece and Cumming (1996) evaluated the cognitive demands of three techniques for improving writing, including dictation and simultaneous oral and visual input. From a developmental perspective, Vieiro and Garcia-Madruga (1997) compared spoken and written summary creation ability of 3rd and 5th graders concluding that the written mode increased literal recall whereas the spoken increased levels of inferences and distortions.

6.6.2   Speech to writing inter-relations and the classroom

These kinds of projects take place largely in the single language context, and more work from the language-learning perspective, such as Haynes (1992) which looks at target-language variability in terms of spoken versus written and native/non-native language users, would be beneficial. Secondly, these studies are generally aimed at the task of writing instruction, and embed discussion of the speech–writing binary within this basic objective. For language pedagogy we may wish to pursue the interrelationship between spoken and written forms in its own right, rather than for the purposes of improving writing alone.

6.7   Summary of central issues discussed in relation to new approaches to speech

There is a growing body of evidence that spoken and written forms of language are processed differently internally, and have different cognitive effects (particularly in relation to memory) when regarded as external modalities.

The evolutionary bias for speech communication and the cognitive challenge which writing presents have implications for second language learning and spoken and written input.

If we cease to see the language faculty as a smoothly homogenous and unitary structure for which the mode of delivery is largely irrelevant several things follow:

• Learning to write a second language may be less directly related to learning to speak a second language than we have assumed.

• Investigations of second language acquisition may need to take into consideration in terms of input and output the implications of separate grammatical organisation of spoken and written forms in the brain.

- If generated directly from the semantic level, the written form may have greater importance for language learning than previously thought and the relations between first and second language writing may be a fruitful avenue for further research.

- The presentation of written and spoken forms can affect the way information is processed and remembered and further work in this area generally, as well as in terms of classroom management, may be beneficial.

- Finally, while not suggesting that unitary concepts such as universal grammar are significantly challenged by findings and suggestions such as those presented here, the role of mode, and in particular the status of speech in language learning, is one to be pursued.

- Given the ideas outlined above, the idea that speech is simply and straightforwardly the partner to writing in the syllabus is not sufficient. This means that there is opportunity for exciting work of a more theoretical orientation on speech than has typically been carried out in applied linguistics.

6.8 Summary

This chapter looked in more detail at the status of speech in applied linguistics, and particularly the interrelations between spoken and written mode. Several pieces of work in related fields – neuro-linguistics, psychology, language processing and so on – were reviewed, and their implications for the role of speech in teaching and learning were highlighted. Two particular aspects – cognitive load and processing, and the use of spoken mode in relation to teaching writing – were given particular attention via two research summaries.

||| Researching speaking

_____

Chapter 7

Classrooms, research and spoken mode

_____

This chapter will . . .

- revise some key features of speech and their implications for research projects;
- address the question of the role of speaking in the classroom and how further research could inform a discussion of this;
- discuss the implications of the imbalance between research into writing versus that into speaking for language teachers and learners.

_____

Quote 7.1 **Yunzhong on the valuing of speech in teaching contexts**

Much has been said during the past few decades on the aural–oral approaches and their obvious advantages in foreign language teaching. Many language teachers and educators have come to regard a command of the spoken language as the most effective means of gaining a fluent reading knowledge and correct speech as the foundation for good writing. They argue that during all our life we shall probably talk more than we shall write. Therefore, speaking a language is far more important that writing it. They have been prone to the belief that learners of a foreign language ought to familiarize themselves with the global structures of the spoken language, within the context of real communication situations where people listen and react.

(Yunzhong, 1985: 12)

7.1   Introduction

Due to the influence of communicative approaches to English language teaching, one of the fundamental tenets of this field nowadays is that it is better for students to talk in the classroom than teachers. This weighting of the speaking towards the students has markedly affected both the nature of classroom management at a global level and the dynamics of micro-interactions between teachers and learners over the last 30 to 40 years.

Activities based around speaking need to be managed and fostered through careful planning and direction by the teacher, and through a choice of suitable tasks to stimulate speech. The need to both engender and manage the vagaries of speech interaction (inherently a more 'messy' process than text-based learning) has brought about a rapid growth in the development of a range of teaching techniques and supporting published materials to help students to speak, in the form of information gap activities, role plays, simulations and games.

The underlying rationale for the activities is that the elicitation of speech *per se* is a desirable end in itself. This in turn is linked to the ideas most famously explored by Krashen (for instance, Krashen, 1982) suggesting that a second language is best acquired by active engagement in meaningful communication (his 'learning–acquisition' hypothesis) and in terms of language comprehension, when learners are exposed to discourse which is slightly beyond that which they can express themselves (his 'input' hypothesis).

The rest of this chapter provides a brief overview of some of the implications of the nature of speech for the classroom and contrasts the treatment of the written and the spoken mode in applied research in of the field of English language teaching.

7.2   Implications of the nature of spoken discourse on teaching speech

When we consider the complex nature of speech interaction, it is perhaps unsurprising that even the most advanced students still feel most at a loss when they are trying to take part in spontaneous, informal conversation in a new language. While the communicative classroom gives abundant opportunity for the student to interact, it is fruitful to raise awareness of the fundamentals of spoken discourse to give students a better understanding of how very different speaking is from the stringing together of grammatically correct (or incorrect) sentences. Language awareness activities based around the norms of spontaneous interaction in the target language can provide both an increased understanding of the problems, pitfalls and skills needed for successful communication with native speakers, and also provide the learner with a meta-language to ask further questions about the difficulties they are encountering.

There are three basic aspects of spontaneous speech which language learners need to be made aware of, and which language teachers may find it helpful to reflect on:

- speaking is fundamentally an interactive task;
- speaking happens under real-time processing constraints;
- speaking is more fundamentally linked to the individual who produces it than the written form is.

These are the elements which stem directly from the way speech is produced and distinguish it from standard written forms. I will discuss each of them further in the following three sub-sections and what they mean for the language learner.

7.2.1 The higher interactive potential of the spoken form than the written

This leads to features not only such as interruptions, corrections and overlaps, but also evidence of speaker co-operation as two or more people seek to speak and understand one another in real time (see Hughes (1996) for further discussions of this).

Learners also need to become aware of the potentially different mechanics of interaction in their own language and the target language (see, for example, Nelson, Mahmood and Nichols (1996), or White (1997)).

Concept 7.1   **The non-transferability of conversational patterns across cultures**

A fundamental issue for the language teacher is the extent to which the norms of a target language's interactions mirror those of the learners' mother tongue. Nelson, Mahmood and Nichols (1996) for example investigated the different ways in which Syrians and Americans respond to compliments. Although there were a number of similarities (for instance mitigating the compliment) there were also some significant differences. Americans were more likely than Syrians to simply say 'thank you'. Syrians were more likely to produce a long or a formulaic response (for instance offering the object of the compliment to the giver of the compliment). Where there is a combination of similarities and differences in the ways that cultures handle conversational functions there can be particular difficulties for the teacher of spoken forms.

7.2.2   The production of speech happens under real-time processing constraints

While the written form can generally be edited, re-written and 'polished', speech – even speech that is prepared in advance – is delivered to the listener with no possibility for the recall of a word or erasure of a grammatical error. The exception, is, of course, spoken discourse which is pre-recorded, and can be re-taped if necessary. However, the greater part of speech, that is, conversational data, is created in real time. This means that speakers tend to use simpler vocabulary, use a higher frequency of co-ordinated clauses, and use many fixed, filler expressions, such as 'you know', 'you see', to buy processing time. Learners need to realise that simple, even repetitive vocabulary is not unacceptable in speech, or rather that they should not spend so long making lexical choices that they lose the chance to speak. Equally, they need to gain a repertoire of natural time buying devices to help them plan and process their discourse more easily.

7.2.3   A strong, perceptible link exists between the deliverer of the discourse and the discourse itself

Spoken discourse reaches the world directly from the human vocal tract. As such it is a less mediated form than the written, which is transferred on to (or with technological advances such as computers and personal communication devices in to) another medium before it is read. Something of this is reflected in the greater evidence of personal involvement shown by the spoken form, for example high frequency of personal pronouns, especially first and second, and verbs showing stance to the topic such as 'think', 'feel', 'believe' and so on.

An awareness of the effects of the interactive, spontaneous and personally oriented nature of speech can, therefore, be of great benefit to learners, both in terms of fluency and appropriacy and also to improve global listening skills. If, however, speech is taught without regard for some of the basic differences brought about by the way it is produced then learners will constantly be striving to speak in the complete, grammatically standard, and impersonal discourse which is untypical of naturally occurring speech.

7.3   Moving towards your own project on spoken discourse

Figures 7.1 and 7.2 present some of the complexities of relationships between practitioners, research, and researchers in applied linguistics. Problems to think about at the outset are listed below.

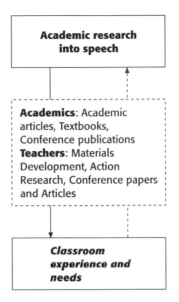

Figure 7.1   Information exchange between academe and classrooms

Global problems for the researcher into speech data

Problem 1 Very few theories of speech per se.

Problem 2 Very few researchers have worked on speech in its own right within applied linguistics.

Problem 3 Within applied linguistic theory 'speech' has often been conflated with 'language' and this can cause difficulties in trying to pin down the exact scope of a research project into the spoken form of language.

Further issues for the researcher into speech

Problem 1 What are you investigating?

Sounds?

Structures or forms?

Discourse?

Problem 2 What theoretical background can I use?

Theories of speech production?

Theories of speech processing?

Frameworks from discourse analysis or conversation analysis?

Problem 3 For language pedagogy, what is the target spoken form?

What dialect form shall I teach?

What model of correctness, if any, will I use?

What model of pragmatic or cultural behaviour will I use?

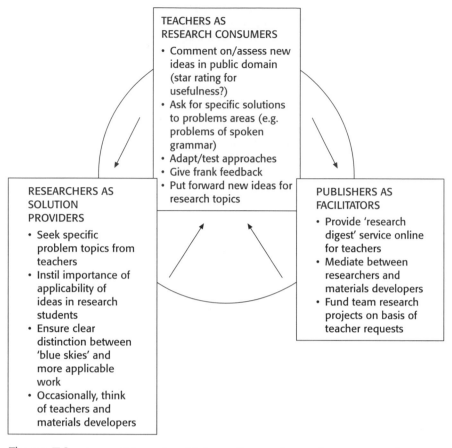

Figure 7.2 **A possible cycle of information exchange between teachers, researchers and publishers**

Problem 4 What are the most appropriate research methods to investigate speech?

Quantitative and/or experimental?

Qualitative and/or integrative?

7.4   Sources of inspiration for research

7.4.1   Personal experience of the profession

A research topic may grow from a problem, question or challenge you meet in your working life. This could relate to your students' progress in their speaking abilities, the dynamics of interactions between them, confusion over who is allowed to speak at a given point, or their own questions to you about speaker dynamics or conversation.

You may find it helpful to keep a research questions notebook to hand at the early stages of a research project and jot down your queries and thoughts about these at the end of a working day. This will be a good source of practically oriented research questions and looking back at the real-world questions which prompted you to begin can help with motivation as the research project develops.

An example of the kind of research which can grow from a problem experienced in a working context can be found in Tyler, Jeffries and Davies (1988).

> **Quote 7.2** Tyler, Jeffries and Davies on a problem arising in spoken academic discourse
>
> Communication problems surrounding the spoken academic discourse of teachers who are non-native speakers of English are a growing concern at US universities. This paper presents partial results of an analysis of the videotaped teaching demonstrations of 18 Korean and Chinese graduate students at the University of Florida. The analysis was carried out within an integrative discourse framework, that is, one which considers the interrelatedness of various levels of linguistic organisation.
>
> (Tyler, Jeffries and Davies, 1988: 101)

When it comes to presenting the research to a reader, these kinds of real-world difficulties give a sense of urgency and interest to the material and can help in particular with the introduction sections of the text.

7.4.2   Developments in the profession

Inspiration for research topics can also be drawn from broader issues outside the classroom which are seen as influencing the profession as a whole.

A broad topic which you might want to pursue might be the changing role of the teacher in the communicative classroom and how this is reflected in teacher talk. In terms of teacher development you may wish to investigate how teacher trainers relate to novice teachers and conduct an ethnographic survey of their interactions. In general, these kinds of topics are most suited to the experienced professional teacher who wants to reflect on the skill of speaking within broader issues which they have seen alter their working lives.

> **Quote 7.3** Hoey on the teaching profession and spoken discourse
>
> Why should a language teacher be concerned with the working of spoken discourse? Certainly not because the learner's syllabus needs to be augmented by explicit introduction to discourse analysis. . . . The real reason that language teachers should consider how discourses are organised is that it will help them to judge better the effectiveness of what they are doing. . . . If the teacher knows what a natural conversation involves, he or she will be in a better position to assess whether their learners are succeeding in developing the conversational skills that they need in order to be effective speakers of the target language.
>
> (Hoey, 1991: 66)

7.4.3 Social or pragmatic issues

Topics for research can also arise from very general matters relating to the norms of conversation. In the early stages of a written introduction to a research paper it is quite common for researchers to relate their specific topic to a real-world issue of some kind, which even the non-specialist can understand, and then to use this as a lead into the specific more academic topic under consideration.

> **Quote 7.4** Eisenstein and Bodman on cross-cultural norms of thanking
>
> Most native speakers of English on a conscious level associate the expression of gratitude with the words 'thank you'; however, they are unaware of the underlying complex rules and the mutuality needed for expressing gratitude in a manner satisfying to both the giver and recipient.
>
> (Eisenstein and Bodman, 1993: 64)

7.4.4 Published research and theory

A very common source of questions for the new researcher is existing work and theory. This is perhaps the most frequent technique by which an academic presents a topic as having relevance to fellow academics. For the novice academic providing clear links between previous work and your own also shows that you have carried out sufficient background research into your topic to be certain that what you are doing is not simply a repe-

> **Quotes 7.5 and 7.6** Two examples of researchers linking the inspiration for their work to previous studies
>
> Another focus of our research has been on how Americans and Japanese perform such speech acts with status unequals. This question was asked because it is generally claimed that Japanese are very conscious of social status while Americans are relatively less status-conscious. Ide (1989) for example, argues.... Similarly, Matsumoto (1989) argues...
>
> (Takehashi and Beebe, 1993: 139)
>
> Previous studies into non-native speaker interlanguage are dominated by a focus on the variation between correct vs. incorrect target language forms (Tarone, 1975, 1988; Tarone and Parrish, 1988; Schachter, 1986; Ellis 1986, 1987; Ellis and Roberts, 1987; Preston, 1989). We must distinguish between these studies of interlanguage *variation* and the study of target language *variability* in the discourse on non-native speakers, which is the topic of this paper.
>
> (Haynes, 1992: 43)

tition of the work of someone else. For this reason the unproven researcher may have to insert higher numbers of references in their literature review than a more seasoned academic.

Where the primary aim of research is to build on previous work the researcher has to be particularly careful to show the novelty and interest of the work being presented. That is to say, if the object of the research is not to solve a real-world problem or to investigate the impacts of developments in the profession, then the value of the work has to be established in some other way. Traditionally in academic settings the appropriacy of a piece of research can be established by showing how it grows out of previous work in the field, and is fulfilling some need in relation to work done before. A good place to look for ideas for research topics is, therefore, in the discussion/conclusion sections of articles you read as background to your own work. Conventionally, the academic writer will show that they are aware of the limitations of their present work by noting what further work could be carried out in the area, and this can help you to focus on a topic of your own.

Chapter 8

Research project ideas and frameworks

This chapter will...

- introduce a number of research projects which have already been carried out on spoken discourse;
- describe further related projects which could be carried out into spoken discourse;
- discuss the research approaches and frameworks for these projects.

8.1 Introduction

The projects selected here for summary show different approaches to moving from speech data towards generalisations which can be used either in wider descriptions of spoken discourse, or applied in the classroom.

Another central concern of this book has been the extent to which research into speech data is actually investigating the nature of speech or investigating some other factor. It is interesting that, although all eight projects I describe are based on spoken data, few see a need to question some of the fundamental ideas about speech or express a need for a research agenda on the topic of speech in its own right.

In each case, therefore, I have included some further topics for research which could grow naturally from the findings described, and also one or two more 'distant' research questions which address the issue of how these results might relate to bigger questions about spoken discourse. Each study also has one related 'reader project' described after it with more detailed instructions about how it might be carried out.

8.2   Projects on oral interaction: a discourse analysis approach and an experimental approach

The first pair of studies I describe both ask a question relating to how far the discourse they are analysing relates to 'typical' speech. The first takes a discourse analysis perspective on what happens in a test interview situation and how this matches up with spontaneous conversational data. The second takes a more experimental approach to the question of how different age groups in a population carry out spoken interaction.

8.2.1   Study 1: A comparison of spoken interaction under test conditions and spontaneous conversation

Research summary: Re-analysing the OPI [Oral Proficiency Interview]: How much does it look like natural conversation? (Johnson and Tyler, 1998)

Marysia Johnson and Andrea Tyler (Johnson and Tyler, 1998) examined the nature of the oral proficiency interview (OPI) used in a number of government institutions in the USA as well as Educational Testing Service (ETS) and the American Council on the Teaching of Foreign Languages (ACTFL). They analysed what they felt to be a typical example of the OPI – a video used to train examiners of a Korean woman being interviewed by two experienced US examiners, one male and one female. Their aim was to compare the interactions in this interview with prototypical features of spontaneous spoken exchanges as highlighted in a cross-section of discourse and conversational analysis research.

The features they examined in detail were:

Turn-taking ('In normal conversation, we expect turn order, length of turns, and turn distribution to be unspecified prior to the exchange. Once the conversation is under way, we expect to see aspects of collaboration and negotiation in construction of the emerging topic' – Johnson and Tyler, 1998: 34)

Adjacency pairs ('One systematic feature of conversational structure that does provide a kind of predictability is the regular occurrence of ordered sequences produced by different speakers. . . . Perhaps the most prototypical adjacency pair is the question–response sequence' – Johnson and Tyler, 1998: 31–32)

Topic nomination ('In natural conversation, topic emerges spontaneously. . . . According to Jones and Gerard (1967) . . . one expects roughly balanced distribution among participants in naturally occurring conversation in terms of initiation of topic as well as turns at talk, length of turn and speaker selection' (Johnson and Tyler, 1998: 32))

Other features of conversational involvement (e.g. displaying interestedness, evaluating interlocutors' contributions).

Johnson and Tyler describe significant disparities between the OPI and key indicators typical of natural conversational discourse. They conclude: 'The analysis of this model OPI interview shows that salient features of natural conversation involved in turn-taking and negotiation of topic are not present' (Johnson and Tyler, 1998: 47). The examiners responded to the interviewee in ways which would be unacceptable in natural conversational contexts, for example, ignoring most of the questions from the candidate or openly challenging the candidate's point of view.

Ideas for further work

1. Ideas close to the research:

- Johnson and Tyler acknowledged that since their analysis was based on a single interview, further work on different examples of the same kind of test would be beneficial. Therefore, a straightforward project would be one based on the question of how typical this example really is of the OPI together with an analysis of data from a much wider range of interviews.

- A second style of project would be one which looked at a variety of oral assessment formats and held them up against spontaneous conversational data in the same way that Johnson and Tyler did for the OPI. The research question here would be 'How far can any oral assessment format permit the display of natural interactive conversational features?'

- Johnson and Tyler's example could also be emulated in terms of an action-research project designed to assess student group interactions or teacher–student interactions in the classroom context, again to see how these measure up against conversational norms. The question here might be 'How far am I fostering features of natural, spontaneous interaction in my classroom?'

2. Ideas further from the research:

- The fundamental assumption in Johnson and Tyler (1998) is that discrepancies between the features of language produced under oral assessment conditions and natural interaction bring into question the validity of the test. An interesting research question, therefore, is whether this is true. That is to say, a more theoretical research paper might explore whether a test could act as a reliable measure of oral proficiency, despite not reflecting 'natural' interaction.

- Discrepancies between the OPI and natural interactive data may be a result of the inherent power imbalance which underpins the assessment event. It would be interesting, therefore, to examine speech genres in the target language which are perhaps closer to the OPI, for example, job interviews and see how far the OPI deviates from the norms of these.

Reader project 8.1

Initial research questions:
How natural is the turn taking in my students' conversation?
Do they realise how appropriate turn-taking affects spoken interactions?

Outcome relevant to teaching:
Evidence to show the learner that their conversational success is not entirely due to their grammatical knowledge or their vocabulary in the target language.

Data gathering:
Ask a small number of your most fluent and confident students (2–3) to record themselves in as many of the spoken encounters they have in the target language as possible during a seven-day period.
Ask them to rate each conversation on a scale of 1–5, according to how successful they felt the interaction was (1 – unsuccessful; 5 = successful). Do not explain any further criteria at this stage, or what *you* mean by successful.

Data analysis:
Transcribe the highest and lowest scoring encounters.
Analyse the interactions, paying particular attention to the following:

Does the learner initiate turns appropriately?

Does the learner respond to initiations appropriately?

Does the learner notice turn-relevant points in the other speaker's discourse (these will differ from language to language, but in English will be signalled by downward intonation and brief pausing)?

Does the learner 'take the floor' smoothly, and/or interrupt politely?

Does the learner speak too much? Too little?

Measure your analysis against your learners' scoring of the encounters. Do these results give you any data to help explain to the student why their conversations were difficult?

8.2.2   Study 2: Investigating the effects of age and education on speech production

---

Research summary: 'Adult spoken discourse: the influences of age and education' (Mackenzie, 2000)

This study looked at the oral interactions and oral picture descriptions of 189 adults within three age ranges: 40–59 (middle aged); 60–74 (young elderly); 75–88 (old elderly). The reason the author was interested in differences between the language performance of these three age groups is that in assessing the speech behaviour of any individual (for instance, after a stroke) little previous work had been done to show what was actually 'normal' for someone more senior. Mackenzie states: 'The conversation interaction of the very old was characterised by ambiguous referencing, verbosity, inappropriate topic change and failure to observe accepted turn-taking rules. When these same features are observed in the speech of those with known brain damage, especially involving the right hemisphere, they have often been regarded as pathological, this judgement being made without adequate comparative normative data being available' (Mackenzie, 2000: 281–282).

Inclusion criteria:
As well as the three age ranges noted above, and three categories of educational background being used (school leaving at minimal age (14–15), school leaving certificate level; and higher (University level) education) the following criteria were used by Mackenzie:

Aged between 40 and 88

English as first language

No reported history of psychiatric or neurological disease, e.g. stroke, Parkinson's disease, dementia

Right-handed

Hearing adequate for conversational purposes and listening to taped material (with hearing aid worn if required)

Vision adequate for picture material and 'large size' book style print (with glasses worn if required) (Mackenzie, 2000: 271)

Assessment criteria for the conversational ability of the subjects were based on five parameters rated 1–5 with 5 being 'normal':

Conversational initiation (shared responsibility versus passivity)

Turn taking (co-operation in sharing responsibility versus domination or lengthy silences)

Verbosity (efficient and to the point versus too much peripheral detail/repetition)

Topic maintenance (sustained, relevant, clearly connected contributions versus ignoring a topic introduced by a participant or introducing a new topic without sufficient 'linking/bridging')

Referencing (clarity in referring to people and events versus lack of relevant prior information, necessitating 'guesswork' on part of listener)

Subjects in the 'old elderly' age group 'were inclined to verbosity, failure to maintain topic, poor turn taking and unclear referencing' (Mackenzie, 2000: 279). Level of education and gender did not affect conversational performance (although in a picture description task those educated to minimal level tended to give shorter and less-elaborated descriptions). Mackenzie suggests that 'awareness of the effects of advancing age and limited education may facilitate successful communication for all who communicate with the public in a professional capacity' (Mackenzie, 2000: 269).

Ideas for further work

1. Ideas close to the research:

   - The issue of what constitutes 'normal' conversation at different stages in an individual's life could be investigated further, particularly in relation to individual differences between speakers. Mackenzie notes that among the 'old elderly' there were several exceptions to the rule (for example, around 50 per cent of them achieving maximum scores for referencing and topic maintenance). What factors influence the ability to maintain these skills in later life?
   - This framework could be adapted to investigate how these results relate to conversational performance by different age groups in a second language context.

2. Ideas further from the research:

   - The underlying assumption behind this work is that conversational norms persist through time, but interlocutors deteriorate. A more challenging view would be that attitudes to conversational norms are not neutral, but are seen through the eyes of largely middle-class, professional, people of working age. The research question here would be to ask, 'By whose norms do we judge conversational appropriacy?'
   - Similarly, Mackenzie notes that conversation with peers may not be the same as that between 'old elderly' with younger interlocutors (Mackenzie, 2000: 279). This raises a very interesting version of the 'Observer's paradox' given that we are not told the age of the assessor participating in the conversation used as the basis for analysis with the subjects. A potential research question here would be, 'Is interaction between "old elderly" interlocutors the same as interaction between this group and younger interlocutors?'

Reader project 8.2

Initial research questions:
How do Mackenzie's findings about the conversational styles of the elderly relate to second language learning?

Outcomes relevant to the language classroom:
If age affects conversational ability in a first language it should also be taken into account in the second language context.

(This project would lend itself to a more library based and/or theoretical approach.)

Library work:
Using some of the bibliographic resources detailed in Chapter 10 carry out a library search on the topic of language learning and age.

Remember that your main aim is not simply to describe previous work on age and language learning, but to think carefully about how Mackenzie's findings might affect second language learning.

Organise your notes under broad headings such as: references to age and language learning ability generally; references to age and conversational style; references to second language learners and conversational styles (do not worry if you cannot find references after a thorough library search – this means that you are homing in on a topic which is genuinely under-researched).

Planning your research paper:
Keep in mind your central question which is whether Mackenzie's work is relevant to second language contexts.

Brainstorm a list or a 'mind map' of the ways in which the results could be useful (for instance, if we have a clearer idea of what is 'normal' conversationally among different age groups, we may understand conversational difficulty or differences better and help learners through this knowledge).

Repeat the process considering the ways in which Mackenzie's results would be difficult to apply to the second language learning context, or perhaps less relevant (for example, are there too many other factors in the second language context which could account for conversational differences (culture and first language)?)

Drafting your research paper:
By this stage you should have a clearer idea of to what extent you feel that Mackenzie's work is relevant to the second language context. The structure of your paper will reflect this.

If on balance you think the findings are relevant and useful, the main direction of your argument and the examples and references you use will support this.

If on the other hand, you think the findings are flawed, irrelevant or otherwise difficult to apply to the second language learning context your argument will be structured to reflect this and further references will be brought in, if possible, to add strength to your point of view.

Hint: Re-read the description of the position paper in Chapter 5, Section 5.2.3.

8.3 Projects on one particular spoken discourse feature: an action-research approach and a conversation analysis approach

The two projects described in this section both deal with repetition. This is an aspect of spontaneous speech which in 'deficiency' models of spoken discourse have been seen as problematic, especially when compared to the written mode. However, in their different ways both these projects suggest that there may be essential functional characteristics of repetition which are of interest not only in their own right, but also in the classroom.

8.3.1 Study 3: An action-research project on conversational 'shadowing' between speakers

Research summary: 'Exploring conversational shadowing' (Murphey, 2001)

Conversational shadowing (i.e. repetition by one speaker of what has just been said by another) happens naturally in L1 context. This project looked at what happens when L2 speakers shadow L1 speakers. The learners in question were first year Japanese students of English who were given some explicit instruction in the use of shadowing, and told to practise this technique in as many contexts as possible, whether silently or aloud. A detailed analysis was then made of two of the students paired with two native speakers in mixed dyads (i.e. both NNS spoke with each NS) on topics which were deemed easy and familiar (their favourite place and their daily routine). Each speaker was asked to take the lead in the conversation to begin with and the partner was told to 'shadow' them. Interestingly, one of the NNS partners interpreted this instruction much more strictly than the other and effectively repeated most of what the lead speaker said. Murphey comments that 'her segments lack negotiation or a discourse structure that represents an exchange of ideas. There seems to be little excitement or curiosity about the information' (Murphey, 2001: 136), and later that the second student's version of shadowing which was more selective matches the norms of interaction better. The rapport shown in this selective shadowing led to the initiating speaker feeling that understanding had not taken place when the smooth, selective shadowing and comments from the NNS broke down.

Murphey suggests a number of intriguing potential benefits from using conversational shadowing in the classroom, from lessening the inhibitions of adult learners to increasing fluency and opportunities for natural self correction.

From the process of analysis Murphey suggests three levels of shadowing might be isolated: complete, selective and interactive and that each of these have different benefits.

Ideas for further work

1. Ideas close to the research:

   Murphey suggests several additional research agendas which emerge from his work (Murphey, 2001: 149–150). I list some of them here:

   - What are the advantages and disadvantages of shadowing versus being shadowed by fellow learners or NSs?

   - How can one effectively teach complete shadowing, and then selective and interactive and how does this relate to strategy training?

   - How much practice is necessary before shadowing becomes an automatic strategy?

2. Ideas further from the research:

   - Further work on the use of shadowing in target language contexts is needed together with a more detailed rationale for teaching shadowing techniques.

   - In particular, interesting projects could be carried out on the cross-cultural assumptions of that is a 'normal' or 'effective' level of interaction and meaning negotiation.

   - In terms of introducing the technique into the classroom, care would be needed to establish the precise objectives for the process (i.e. fluency building, conversational confidence building, error correction, interactive skill building).

Reader project 8.3

Initial research questions:
Does shadowing as described by Murphey really increase fluency?

Outcomes relevant to the classroom:
If shadowing can be shown to have significant benefits for the second language learner, similar techniques might be incorporated into teaching speaking more widely and investigated further.

Experimental design:
Decide on your initial framework. For example, decide which kind of shadowing you are going to investigate (complete, selective, interactive), perhaps opting for complete as this is the easiest to explain to the student. Decide what measure of fluency you are going to use. Perhaps use something simple at this stage, such as words per minute.

Plan your experiment on the basis of a control group of language learners and an experimental group with whom the shadowing technique is going to be used. To clarify things, call these Group A and Group B, and define these for yourself and for your eventual reader, so that there is no doubt about the nature of the two groups.

Fix as many of the variables between groups as possible, so that any differences in fluency rates can be laid at the door of the shadowing intervention, rather than being due to other factors.

Remember the pros and cons of size of group in experimental work. The larger the numbers of subjects from whom you gain data, the more convincing your results will be, particularly in statistical terms. The smaller the numbers involved the more manageable the project will be, and you will be able to investigate or take into account learner-specific factors which may have influenced their progress.

Consider the following factors when you are trying to match groups of learners: age, gender, language level, nationality, and other significant factors which might affect language progress, for example, the teacher and materials used. If it is impossible to match every aspect of the two groups (and it very often is), do not try to hide this fact, but discuss the difficulty and its implications somewhere in your research report, for instance in the methods section, or in the discussion and interpretation of results.

The experiment:
Test the fluency levels of the students involved in Group A and Group B according to the criterion or criteria you have chosen to work with (for example, words per minute).

Test the fluency levels again at the end of the experimental period.

In between the two tests Group A should follow a standard syllabus. Group B should follow the same course with the exception that they should be exposed to the shadowing techniques at points in the course when the focus of the speaking class is on fluency.

Hint Do not give the shadowing work to an extra activity on top of the work done by Group A. If you do this, then any gains in fluency scores could be attributed to extra class time, rather than the effect of the technique itself.

8.3.2   Study 4: A conversational analytical study of repetition by individuals

Research summary: 'Repetition in conversation: A look at "first and second sayings"' (Wong, 2000)

Jean Wong takes issue with the idea that repetition within an individual's speech in conversation is something negative or to be seen as to be eliminated from learners' discourse. In fact, her suggestion is that this is a highly effective technique used by speakers to 'keep the floor' as they evaluate whether their interlocutor has understood them, expand or explain a point, and then resume their discourse before another speaker can break in.

Wong uses a conversation analysis approach to describe the phenomenon and bases her analysis around the units 'first saying + insertion + second saying' where the first and last unit are nearly identical and joined by a 'parenthetical' remark and concludes:

'Instances of first and second sayings reflect a phenomenon of talk and social organization that might be referred to as unspoken repair (or unspoken repair projection). The second saying preempts [sic] actual repair, the insertion being viewed as a potential trouble source on which repair could be initiated.' (Wong, 2000: 416)

Wong goes on to report her analysis of transcripts of second language users and comments on the lack of this kind of phenomenon in their discourse despite what she calls its 'formal simplicity' (i.e. exact repetition after a self-interrupt). She notes that in strictly conversation analytical terms this absence would not necessarily be noteworthy (i.e. it is a tradition which is interested in 'what is there' and what features the speakers actually use to orient themselves to topics and each other rather than comparing the discourse against a preconceived ideal). However, she also suggests that its lack is an interesting example of how the minutiae of talk can reveal the level of confidence and sense of community that exists between speakers.

Ideas for further work

1. Ideas close to the research:

   - Analyse your own, or your learners' conversation to see whether you use Wong's practice of 'first and second saying'.

   - Set up some informal narrative tasks for your friends (i.e. in a relaxed setting ask for anecdotes about their most exciting holiday, or their most embarrassing moment). Do these speakers pre-empt interruption by repeating themselves?

   - Introduce your learners to the idea of this kind of repetition as a skill and monitor the subsequent their development (or absence) of the technique in their spoken discourse.

2. Ideas further from the research:

   - One feature of the conversation analysis approach is that it draws attention to aspects of talk which are so commonplace as to be unnoticed by and large and then provide a compelling explanation based on the examples analysed. However, stepping out of the CA paradigm it might be salutary to define the scope of the 'first and second saying' more explicitly and then examine a larger sample of the structure to see whether the explanation fits the majority of the examples or whether such repetitions carry out a number of conversational functions.

Reader project 8.4

Initial research question:
How much repetition do learners use in their speech? Do they use this strategically or not?

Outcome for the classroom:
Many learners regard repetition in their spoken discourse as a negative thing. This attitude is strongly influenced by literate views of language which stem from the careful language choices which the written mode permits. Understanding that repetition in oral discourse is not only inevitable in unplanned contexts, but that it can also be used to increase speaking effectiveness may improve learner confidence and fluency.

Data gathering:
Set up tasks in which learners will have the chance to produce both largely monologue (for example, story-telling) and dialogue (for instance, a discussion or debate).

Decide how you are going to define repetition. For example, do the repetitions have to occur directly after one another? Are you going to use the 'First and second saying' model which permits an intervening element? How far apart can elements occur and still be counted as a repetition? Note that in some respects it does not matter how you count repetition, but problems arise if you count repetition differently across different speakers. It makes life much easier to define what you are analysing at the outset.

Record the spoken discourse you are going to analyse, and either transcribe it (if you are carrying out a full research project) or play it back to yourself and make notes (if your aim is more developmental and 'action-research' oriented).

Note the instances of repetition as defined by your research framework.

If there are instances try to categorise them according to speaker purpose. Are repetitions being used effectively? Does the speaker seem confident and comfortable with the amount of repeated material they are using?

If there are no examples, are there places where strategic repetition could have helped the speaker keep the floor or otherwise improved their discourse?

8.4 Projects on oral task difficulty: two approaches to quantifying complexity

8.4.1 Study 5: Oral tasks and their influence on language production

Research summary: 'Quality of language and purpose of task: patterns of learners' language on two oral communication tasks' (Bygate, 1999)

Bygate's fundamental question is 'Are there differences in the grammatical complexity of the learners' oral second language use on two different task types?'. This question was pursued through the analysis of 67 Hungarian secondary school students of similar linguistic ability in English. Two task types were given to them, they self-selected pairs and were tape recorded carrying out the tasks. The tasks chosen were (a) narratives (which the author predicted would call for 'significant imaginative demands, in extended unsupported monologue, which might increase or decrease the complexity of the language' (Bygate, 1999: 194); (b) argumentation (which Bygate suggested 'might provide more scaffolding, both in terms of the dialogic nature of the collaborative talk, which could also lead to greater complexity' (Bygate: 1999: 195)).

In order to measure complexity the following were analysed:

Length of T-units in terms of number of words, reported as the mean per task

Subordination, defined here to include all finite embedded clauses

Proportion of verb arguments (i.e. elements dependent on the verb)

Frequency of verb forms and verb groups

Type of subordination

Results:

The students produced more words per T-Unit in narrative than in argumentation

The higher number of words was not due to subordination, however

Narratives showed higher incidences of verb arguments whereas the argumentation task generated more individual verb forms

Relative clauses were far more common in the narrative tasks than in the argumentation tasks

Bygate concludes that these findings have significant implications for the classroom in terms of the expectations of teachers of the kind of language which will be generated by the different kinds of task: shorter utterances, brainstorming style utterances, echoic interactions and a wider variety of verb forms in argumentation tasks as opposed to longer, nominally elaborated and sustained speech in the narrative tasks.

Ideas for further work

1. Ideas close to the research:

   • This is an interesting project quite apart from its results as it is a good example of the difference between the research procedure and presentation. Although the measures of complexity are listed at the start of the article as if they were pre-established, it becomes clear that these were developed during the research process in order to investigate different aspects, or possible explanations for the main data (on T-Units) in more detail. It would be interesting to duplicate the project using the full set of measures from the outset.

2. Ideas further from the research:

  • Although 'oral proficiency' is mentioned in the article, the question of how complexity and 'proficiency' interact is not considered in detail. This would be a very fundamental question for research into speech, and is dealt with again in Study 6.

Reader project 8.5

Initial research question:
Would it matter if first language speakers did not show the same kinds grammatical variation between tasks as Bygate's learners?

Outcomes for the classroom:
Many of the research projects reported here analyse first language oral production as a model for second language production. A central question, therefore, is how far learner spoken data and first language speaker data overlap.

This project is intended to be more theoretically oriented than others mentioned and should take the form of an extended essay or dissertation with suitable references and development of an argument towards a conclusion. *Hint:* Adapt the research processes outlined in Reader project 8.2.

8.4.2   Study 6: Oral tasks and their difficulty

In his book *A Cognitive Approach to Language Learning* (1998) Peter Skehan summarised a number of pieces of research into the factors influencing task difficulty. His table has been often repeated and forms the basis of several projects.

A recent article again based on the dimensions represented by Skehan and which is particularly useful as a starting point for further work on the idea of oral task difficulty is Iwashita, McNamara and Elder (2001).

Table 8.1   **Factors influencing task difficulty**

Easier condition	Harder condition
Small number of participants, elements	*Greater number of participants, elements*
Concrete information and task	*Abstract information and task*
Immediate, here-and-now information	*Remote, there-and-then information*
Information requiring retrieval	*Information requiring transformation*
Familiar information	*Unfamiliar information*

Source: Based on Skehan (1998: 174, Table 7.2).

Research summary: 'Can we predict task difficulty in an oral proficiency test? Exploring the potential of an Information-Processing Approach' (Iwashita *et al.*, 2001)

This study addresses the following question: Are different task characteristics and performance conditions (involving assumed different levels of cognitive demand) associated with different levels of fluency, complexity, or accuracy in test candidate responses? . . . We found that task performance conditions in each dimension failed to influence task difficulty and task performance as expected. We discuss implications for the design of speaking assessments and broader research (Iwashita, McNamara and Elder, 2001: 401–2).

The researchers analysed oral narrative data from students elicited from picture stimuli.

Four dimensions were investigated with the assumptions about task difficulty based on previous research evidence:

Perspective (story told from own perspective – easier task; story told from someone else's point of view – more difficult task)

Immediacy (with the pictures – easier task; without the pictures – more difficult task)

Adequacy (complete set of pictures – easier task; incomplete set of pictures – more difficult task)

Planning time (3.5 minutes planning time – easier task; 0.5 minutes planning time – more difficult task)

The hypotheses associated with these dimensions were that candidates' narratives created under less-difficult task conditions will be more accurate, more fluent and less complex, measured as follows:

Fluency (measured in terms of reformulations, false starts, repetitions and hesitations and pauses, divided by the total amount of speech)

Accuracy (percentage of error free clauses in total number of clauses)

Complexity (number of clauses divided by the number of c-units, i.e. a simple/independent clause and any associated subordinate clause)

Results:
Interestingly, the hypotheses were, in general, not supported by the results. The only clear-cut finding was that, counter to the assumption of the researchers (but in line with some earlier research on the topic), the narratives told without the aid of pictures tended to be more accurate than those told with the aid of them.

Ideas for further work

1. Ideas close to the research:

   One of the key ideas which this research is investigating is whether it is possible to define speaking tasks in terms of difficulty in such a way as to provide a consistent framework to assess oral ability. The findings showed such little consistent variation that the authors concluded that the present study could not support that conclusion. However they suggest a number of possible further avenues for research:

- Using richer/more diverse input as prompts for narrative (e.g. dialogues from television 'soaps').

- Using other tape-based tasks which can be varied systematically (e.g. map and direction tasks).

- Finding better ways to put into practice task difficulty dimensions (the authors question whether their use of first person/third person perspective was really a adequate reflection of the dimension of 'Familiarity of Information' as they hoped it might be).

- Combining greater elaborateness of task and increased planning time to see if this increased accuracy and fluency.

- Considering whether classroom and test conditions significantly alter the cognitive demands of oral narrative ('For example, a focus on accuracy may be paramount in the testing situation regardless of the conditions under which the task is performed, and this in turn may affect the fluency and complexity of candidates' speech' (Iwashita, McNamara and Elder, 2001: 431)).

2. Ideas further from Iwashita *et al.* (2001)

- A comparison of the measures of accuracy, fluency and complexity with speech data in the target language by native speakers produced under the same conditions.

Reader project 8.6

Initial research question:
Is Iwashita *et al.*'s suggestion that oral narratives under test conditions will be more accurate than those under classroom conditions true?

Outcomes for the classroom:
The suggestion that students' oral performance as measured by accuracy may vary predictably according to test versus other conditions has interesting implications for the teacher trying to assess oral progress.

Carrying out this project would involve replicating Iwashita *et al.*'s method as closely as possible whilst varying the context in which the narratives were carried out: test and classroom conditions. This could be achieved by splitting the subjects between two groups one of which carried out the task under test conditions and the other which carried out the task as part of a lesson. A second method would be to ask the same students to carry out the task twice, once under test conditions and once not.

In the case of the first approach, particular care would be needed to match the students in the two groups for the reasons of comparability described under Reader project 8.3. If the same students were given the narrative task on two different occasions the effects of (a) duration between the two task performances (i.e. if too great a time period is left, general language improvement may occur); (b) the effect of task familiarity.

8.5   Projects on differences between mode: two experimental approaches

8.5.1   Study 7: A project on spoken mode and its role in teaching writing skills

To exemplify the role speaking can play in techniques for teaching other skills, Reece and Cumming (1996) will be summarised, and then their conclusions adapted for possible research in the second language classroom.

Whereas traditionally the communicative approach or direct methods have seen speech production as an end in itself, and writing a natural outcome of gaining the spoken form, recent work on mode suggests that combining spoken and written forms in specific ways can be beneficial, particularly in terms of improving writing ability and/or recall. For example, Janssen, van Waes and van den Bergh (1996) investigated the role of speech in terms of how far it can provide direct evidence of cognitive processes underlying writing via 'thinking aloud' data. Daly-Jones *et al.* (1997) suggest clear communicative advantages for speech-and-pen messages over single mode messages. On the developmental front, Jones (1998) investigated the benefits for young writers of software which provides immediate oral feedback (i.e. automated reading aloud of sentences written by the child), concluding that the length, complexity and cohesion of the writing improves via such techniques.

Research summary: 'Evaluating speech-based composition methods' (Reece and Cumming, 1996)

Reece and Cumming (1996) begin from the assumption that writing is a cognitively difficult task. They suggest that whereas adults have 'automated' several of the lower level tasks such as punctuation and spelling, children find these aspects particularly challenging. Previous work had suggested that planning could relieve some of the processing demands during writing. In addition, the authors point to the use of dictation as a means of overcoming some of the cognitive load which children find in the mechanics of writing. The authors review previous work on dictation which suggests that the benefits for young writers of using spoken mode are greater than for adults (who may feel the lack of the visual representation needed for re-reading – a process seen in effective writers as they write). To overcome this problem Reece and Cumming proposed the 'Listening Wordprocessor' which would permit near simultaneous text production on screen via speech input from the composer of the text.

The authors subsequently designed a series of studies which would test the efficacy of three potential aids to composition: unplanned dictation; pre-planned dictation and the 'Listening Wordprocessor' (LWP). These were analysed in relation to straightforward writing via normal means, and without pre-planning. Planned dictation scored more highly in the results (both for adults and children) than either unplanned writing or planned writing. For young learners the LWP generally produced the highest quality of texts, and was of particular benefit to poor writers. Interestingly, there appeared to be no great additional benefit when pre-planning was introduced prior to use of the LWP.

As was the case with the work on mode and memory, or mode and cognitive load, this type of research has clear implications for the use of spoken mode in second language learning contexts.

Ideas for further work

1. Ideas close to the research:

- An initial project would be to carry out a very similar experiment using the same age groups and methods, but with subjects who were second language learners. The underlying question here would be are similar improvements to writing seen in second language learners by means of oral delivery of the written material?

- The results of this kind of work may suggest that learners with different writing systems benefit from multi-modal approaches to differing extents. Therefore, further work could be carried out into the influence of script and dictation techniques for writing improvement.

- The rapid development of new technologies of speech recognition software may permit relatively easy experimentation in the classroom of the effects of different modes. A classroom-based study would investigate the progress of control and experimental groups of second language writers with the latter being given instruction in the use of voice-to-text software.

- A further question would be whether the effects of a 'real' scribe taking down oral material to be represented on-screen are different from those of voice-recognition software doing the same job.

> **Reader project 8.7**
>
> *Research question:*
> Do weak writers in a second language gain similar benefits to those outlined in Reece and Cumming's experiment (i.e. the reduction of cognitive demand by the use of oral delivery of material on to screen)?
>
> *Project design:*
> Adapt the method outlined in Reece and Cumming using equipment available in your context. This could be a simple replication of their 'Listening Wordprocessor' or the use of more recent voice-to-text software.
>
> Assess the quality of the writing before and after a period of exposure to this technique. Alternatively, carry out an experiment and control group investigation as described under Research project 8.3.
>
> *Hint:* In the second language context there may be additional complexities due to difficulties in recognising items produced orally by language learners, particularly when speech recognition software is used. This would need to be taken into account in the research design and the discussion.

8.5.2   Study 8: Relative processing demands of speech and writing

A number of the articles reviewed in the previous parts of this book have suggested that there might be strong differences in the cognitive demands of speech and writing, and that these may be important in relation to language production and language development. Therefore, one possible thread of research is an investigation of the role of mode and its processing demands in the second language classroom in some more detail. Most of the research reviewed above has been carried out in the first or single language context, and so an initial point is that there is room for fruitful work in relation to second language learning.

Two areas in particular point to interesting potential research on the role of speaking in improving specific aspects of language learning. The first is in relation to memory and language processing, the second in relation to using speech specifically to improve writing ability.

As an example of the this aspect, Bourdin and Fayol (1996) will be summarised, and then used as a basis for extending their research conclusions into the second language teaching and learning context.

> **Research summary: 'Mode effects in a sentence production span task' (Bourdin and Fayol, 1966)**
>
> Bourdin and Fayol (1996) investigated the relative cognitive load of speaking and writing. They were particularly interested in whether there were differences between children and adults in this respect. They designed an experiment in which people were asked to memorise a list of isolated

words, shown them on cards and spoken aloud, and then to produce (in the correct order) a sentence for each word. Half the sentences were spoken and half written.

The underlying assumption, based on previous research on memory, was that there is a 'pay off' between cognitive processing and working memory. The authors suggest that 'if the activities involved in writing are cognitively more costly than those involved in speaking, more resources will be devoted to the processing function in the written mode than in the oral mode. As a consequence fewer resources will be left for storage in the written than in the oral mode.' That is, the higher the cognitive demands of the mode the worse the performance of the memory task because of the amount of effort expended just in producing the language. In particular, in this paper they predicted that children would find the cognitive challenge of speaking easier than writing when compared to adults.

Interestingly, according to their results, in the case of adults, the written mode appeared to improve recall rather than hinder it. In children below the age of around 7 results were consistent with their prediction, i.e. these children could recall and produce sentences for more words via oral mode than written. While the authors discuss the possible reasons for these results in some detail, they do not explicitly address the fact that adults appear to find spoken tasks *more* challenging than written. You might predict, for instance, that once writing had become 'natural' to the adult (i.e. as natural as speech to the child) there would simply be equal results for processing load between the two forms.

Ideas for further work and a technique to generate potential research questions

Consider the results of the Bourdin and Fayol paper outlined in the research summary box. Take two pieces of paper and on the first write 'Teaching young learners' and on the other 'Teaching adult learners'. In the middle of the first write the key point from Bourdin and Fayol (1996) about children under seven and the cognitive load of writing. In the middle of the second sheet write a similar summary for adult learners about the spoken mode. Draw a circle around each of these statements, and spend five minutes on each, drawing lines from the inner circle with any question, points, implications that occur to you about the findings.

There are a number of further points and questions which could be raised and/or used as the starting point for further research:

- Do young *second* language learners also find speaking less challenging than writing? Is it to the same degree?

- Are there significant differences between different first languages in terms of the cognitive load of speaking versus writing, for example learners with first languages that have non-alphabetic writing systems?

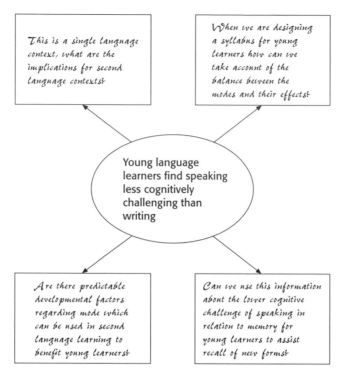

Figure 8.1

- Traditionally there is a balance in the syllabus between the skills, does this balance take enough account of differences in processing load?
- Should younger learners be given more support for their writing, possibly using spoken mode devices (see next research review section)?
- What are the implications for the timing of the introduction of structures and elements in the syllabus?
- SLA studies suggest a progression of acquired forms, will this be identical across both modes?

Do the same thing with the suggestion that adults may find speaking more cognitively challenging. Again there are a number of further comments and questions which can be asked in relation to this work, for example:

- Is it possible to reduce the cognitive load for adult learners by incorporating written mode cues or 'scaffolding'?
- Is the cognitive load the same across different speaking contexts?
- In contexts where there is greater focus on accuracy, do adults find speech production more of a challenge?
- Are there affective factors which alter adults' capacity to speak as opposed to children?

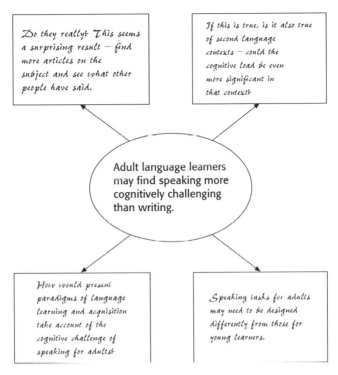

Figure 8.2

- In terms of tasks depending on recall, will adults fare better when written or bi-modal (see below) approaches are taken?

Reader project 8.8

Research question:
How well will second language learners perform Bourdin and Fayol's recall task?

Implications for the classroom:
There is a growing interest in the cognitive demands of classroom tasks, but mode has not been investigated fully.

Project design:
Replicate Bourdin and Fayol's experiment as closely as possible. Whereas their interest was in differences between children and adults, this project would be designed to carry out the task with adult language learners in the target language and compare the findings with those for adults in the Bourdin and Fayol experiment.

IV Resources and further information

Chapter 9

Research borders and boundaries

This chapter will...

- provide indications of the relationship between research into speaking and other Applied Linguistics disciplines;
- revisit some of the applications of research which were dealt with in the opening chapters, and give indications of how different areas influence one another.

9.1 Introduction

As noted in many places in this book, there has been remarkably little work either in linguistics or applied linguistics into speaking as a unified language faculty. Therefore, to a certain extent this book has needed to draw together work from different fields and at different levels within the skill of speaking to attempt to present a useful picture of research into speech for the applied linguist or teacher interested in working on the skill in its own right. Any unified theory of speaking would need to both bring together, and demarcate itself clearly from, a number of interrelated academic disciplines, from communication studies to corpus linguistics. We do not as yet have such a theory, nor does the discipline as a whole yet feel any great lack because of this. The growth of insights about the spoken form which are beginning to emerge from work in discourse analysis, conversation analysis, pragmatics, corpus linguistics and neuro-linguistics mean that there is, however, a distinct pressure for more work on the topic, and also a need to make research findings usable by the more applied and pedagogically oriented sections of the linguistics community.

This chapter reviews some of the sister disciplines which are particularly pertinent to research into the faculty of speech, and attempts to show how their insights could relate to a more holistic approach to research into speech. Initially this broadening of the scope of work on spoken data may seem to be unduly far-reaching, making the study of spoken mode a study of global cultural and ethnographic issues, social issues, psychology, biology, as well as the more traditional aspects of research into language, such as phonology, grammar and syntax. However, I have been arguing throughout this book that there is a need to begin to tease out the differences between research into the language faculty and research into the faculty of speech. This can only be done by moving beyond conceptions of speech which remain grounded in strongly text-based approaches to the study of language.

Secondly, the broadening of the base of research into speech does not look as extreme as it might if it is compared with attitudes to research into the written mode. Work on literacy, and particularly that in the field of critical linguistics, has long acknowledged the role of social and cultural factors in writing performance and it is perhaps only the conceptualisation of speech as both natural and the primary form of language which has led to the mode being treated somewhat differently from the written form, and, paradoxically, to the detriment of our understanding of the speech faculty.

9.2 Speaking and ethnographic or cross-cultural studies

At the broadest level, research into speech needs to be informed by the cultural expectations of speakers. Our understanding not only of conversational 'rules' and norms, but also our interpretation of meaning or even individual words is coloured by our (generally unconcious) acceptance of certain fundamental cultural premises.

A better awareness of the potential differences between cultures in ways which affect language behaviour can also imbue research into speech with greater insight and sensitivity. For example, speech rate, intonation, interruption or self-correction, pauses and attitudes to silence may all be areas which a researcher interested in spoken mode would investigate. While within one's own discourse and language community such aspects may have one interpretation, in a different one their implications and effects may also be quite different – the silence which in one culture is uncomfortable or even rude is unproblematic or deferential in another. Awareness of such issues can in themselves provide insights for the researcher into speech, but, more importantly, can raise fundamental questions about the constructs we engage with in dealing with speech phenomena in the research process. Investigations carried out via actual speech data, particularly if quantitatively based, might attempt to answer research questions via inappropriate elements in the discourse if the broader cultural and ethnographic context is not properly understood.

Also of particular interest in this area is the attitude to spoken and written mode, and their relative status in society. The work of Jack Goody on the ethnography of literacy and orality (for instance, 1977, 1987, 2000), or David Olson's work (Olson and Torrance, 1991; Olson, 1996a, 1996b) or Walter Ong (1971, 1982) is seminal in this area.

9.3 Speaking and psycholinguistics

Psycholinguistic studies focus on the relationship between brain, language and behaviour. The tendency has been for links to be investigated between psychological processes and speech behaviour at the level of planning and delivery rather than on wider psychological motivations to speech behaviour, for example how idiolect is affected by emotional or experiential factors. Aspects of speech which the psycholinguist would be interested in revolve around both practical topics such as the relationship between grammar, memory and language processing and, at the more theoretical end of the spectrum, the different levels or hierarchies involved in language production and comprehension, or the links between brain and language acquisition.

9.4 Speaking and neuro-linguistic studies

Neuro-linguistics differs from psycholinguistics in that the focus of research is on the biological and neurological basis of language processing. As such, research into fundamental aspects of speech such as those outlined in Chapter 6 can be investigated within neuro-linguistic frameworks. It is interesting to note how little either psycho- or neuro-linguistics affect mainstream applied linguistics and language teaching, despite a long and reputable research tradition. There is, however, a strong link existing between this field and speech pathology/therapy.

9.5 Speaking and corpus linguistics

Until relatively recently the greatest part of corpus work in linguistics was based on written evidence and overall the balance still remains in favour of the written mode. This is due to the labour-intensive nature of preparing transcribed speech data in comparison with the relative ease, particularly in the age of electronic documentation and scanning, of capturing written material.

However, with a growing interest in speech data and the technological advances offered by powerful personal computers and the internet a large number of projects based on spoken material is being created, and, more importantly, being made generally available to researchers.

There is also a strong relationship developing between particular publishing houses and the creation of different corpora. For instance Collins and the Cobuild Corpus (information at http://titania.cobuild.collins.co.uk/boe.info.html) or Longman and the British National Corpus, or Cambridge University Press and the CANCODE (Cambridge and Nottingham Corpus of Discourse in English) project.

Research into spoken corpora is throwing up many insights about the form, but from the perspective of a unified theory or approach to speech work on corpus linguistics will always tend to isolate the samples of speech data from the original oral/aural channel in which they were produced, and also from the overall context of the discourse.

9.6 Speaking and new technologies

A fast-moving area in recent years has been the development of new technologies which blur or alter the traditional boundaries between spoken and written mode. An excellent overview of human to machine spoken interaction is provided at the MIT website at http://www.sls.lcs. mit.edu/sls/. The aim of such work is for the user to be able to speak to a computer in much the same way as they would to another person, and for the machine to be capable of carrying out the instruction. The major applications of human–machine speech are in mobile telephony (where at the time of writing the capacity for voice-operated commands was already available), internet searching and access, as well as applications in defence and aid for the physically less able.

Chapter 10

Research resources

This chapter will...

- provide a selection of resources for the researcher;
- provide research process summaries in tabular form.

10.1 Traditional library resources

The following central journals in applied linguistics will all contain relevant material on the diverse aspects of spoken language, if not on spoken mode per se:

TESOL Quarterly
Applied Linguistics
ELT Journal
Language Learning
Language Teaching
Linguistics and Education (tends to have a strong interest in literacy practices)

More specialised publications which often contain material of particular relevance to the researcher into spoken mode are the following:

The Annual Review of Applied Linguistics
Issues in Applied Linguistics
Applied Psycholinguistics
Communication Education

Language and Communication

Language Sciences

Language Teaching Research

Journal of Language and Social Psychology

Journal of Speech and Hearing Sciences

Speak Out (newsletter of the special interest group on speech and pronunciation published by IATEFL)

*Language Teaching: the International Abstracting Journal for Language
Teachers and Applied Linguists* (formerly called Language Teaching
Abstracts) is also a useful resource

10.2   Databases and sound archives (both on-line and on CD-ROM)

The development of the internet has meant that access to oral language
data is becoming increasingly easy. As well as the corpora described in
Section 10.3, sound archive material is available at the following sites most
of which provide downloadable sound files, or can provide taped material
for research purposes:

- The Australian Film related sound archive:
  http://www.screensound.gov.au/index.html (mainly relating to film
  and the arts, but including interview material)

- The (British) National Sound Archive:
  http://www.bl.uk/collections/sound-archive/holdings.html (general
  and oral history material, including political history) and
  http://www.bl.uk/collections/sound-archive/accents.html for
  material on British accents and dialects

- The Michigan State University voice library:
  http://www.lib.msu.edu/vincent/ (including web access to samples of
  all US presidents' voices of twentieth century)

- The Webcorp site has both historical and funny examples of speech
  available to download at: http://www.webcorp.com/sounds/index.htm

- The Swiss National Sound Archive of recordings by and about the
  Swiss nation at: http://www.snsa.ch/e/coll.html

- At the time of writing the BBC were providing an excellent site on
  the evolution of the English language which included downloadable
  examples of a cross-section of British voices:
  http://www.bbc.co.uk/radio4/routesofenglish/index.shtml

- The Stanford collection of Sound Recordings:
  http://www-sul.stanford.edu/depts/ars/ars.html
- The Belfer Audio Archive at the University of Syracuse:
  http://libwww.syr.edu/information/belfer/main.htm
- A very varied and downloadable set of spoken English examples
  provided by:
  http://www.alt-usage-english.org/archive/audio_archive.shtml
- The US Library of Congress provides a sound archive reached
  through links from: http://www.loc.gov/
- An excellent set of links on oral history can be found at:
  http://www.essex.ac.uk/sociology/ohs/ohsorgs.html
- A site which incorporates sound clip and sound archive links into an
  EFL context including work on the differences between US and
  British English is: http://clcaston.com/briteng.html

10.3 Speech corpora

There are a growing number of access routes to spoken corpora on
the web. For example, the ICAME website at
http://www.hd.uib.no/icame.html provides sample access to and also sells
CD-ROM versions of the following corpora containing speech data:

- London Lund Corpus
- Lancaster/IBM Spoken English Corpus (SEC)
- Corpus of London Teenage Language (COLT)
- Wellington Spoken Corpus (New Zealand)
- The International Corpus of English–East African component

At Michael Barlow's Aethelstan site (http://www.athel.com/cspa.html) it is
also possible to sample a corpus of professional and academic spoken interactions and buy related software, or find samples of more general spoken
material at http://info.ox.ac.uk/bnc/ in the British National Corpus.

10.4 Societies and organisations

The special interest groups of IATEFL on Research and on Pronunciation can be found at: http://www.iatefl.org/research.htm and
http://members.aol.com/pronunciationsig/

In addition to the general page for TESOL at http://www.tesol.edu/ there is the special interest section on speech and, mainly, pronunciation at: http://www.public.iastate.edu/~jlevis/SPRIS/

10.5   Speech recognition and text-to-speech

Ideas and resources for using speech recognition to help students with disabilities can be found at:
http://www.edc.org/spk2wrt/lab.html
A history of attempts to produce artificial speech can be found at:
http://www.ling.su.se/staff/hartmut/kemplne.htm
An example of a text-to-speech engine in seven languages is available at:
http://www.digalo.com/index.htm

10.6   On-line pronunciation and intonation resources

A large number of useful sites are listed at:
http://www.sunburstmedia.com/PronWeb.html
A site which provides examples of different accents of the British Isles is at:
http://www.phon.ox.ac.uk/~esther/ivyweb/
An easy to navigate and useful site which plays sound-files of common American contractions in speech is at:
http://www.spokenamericanenglish.com/

10.7   Research skills summaries

This section gives a brief overview of some techniques for research and presenting findings.

10.7.1   Research questions

The most common way of shaping research is to found it on a single over-arching question which summarises the main thrust of the project as a whole. Table 10.1 gives some examples of broad research questions which might grow out of some of the articles summarised in Chapter 5.

Table 10.1   **Broad research questions growing out of previous work**

Article	Potential further questions
Liberman (1998)	Is there real evidence for the 'biological advantage of speech over writing/reading' which Liberman takes as a premise?
Dörnyei (1995)	How does difficulty of oral task interact with communicative strategy?
Scollon and Wong-Scollon (1991)	How could these insights affect or impinge on student/teacher discourse or student/student discourse in mixed nationality settings?
Carter and McCarthy (1995)	How and at what level would you introduce the evaluative function of 'tails' to the learner?
Haynes (1992)	How does the concept of 'native speaker variability' affect our overall understanding of target language and/or correctness?
Rapp and Caramazza (1997)	How far are these results limited to the single case analysed?
Osborne (1996)	Are these results reduplicable with different levels of learner?
Lennon (1990)	How far is perception of spoken fluency affected by cultural expectation?
Saffran, Newport and Asin (1996)	What other 'difficult problems encountered in language acquisition' might distributional learning processes account for?

10.7.2   The cycle of research

It is useful to remember that the process of research is cyclical. Priorities and tasks will differ depending on what stage in the cycle the researcher is at.

Table 10.2 **The cycle of research**

Research cycles	Earlier stages	Central stages	Final stages
Think (topic)	Define scope of project for yourself	Re-define scope and topic, re-draft outline	Check and review scope of findings in relation to original aims
↓	↓	↓	↓
Find	Background readings; setting up relevant research questions; carrying out pilot studies	Carry out research activity to investigate topic, conducting surveys, analysing data, detailed readings and argument	Find final references, check references, complete bibliography
↓	↓	↓	↓
Think (audience)	Consider topic, outline and scope in light of assessors of your work (supervisor – journal readership)	Draft chapters or sections aiming for consistency of style and taking into account readership – remember no one will be as familiar with the detail of the work as you are	Review final draft of research text – will it make sense to a reader who has not experienced your research processes? Are there clear linking sections showing the logic and progression of your ideas? Write your introduction and abstract
↓	↓	↓	↓
Present	Present initial ideas	Present drafts to peer review, supervisor review, conferences/ seminars etc.	Submit final draft (generally there will be a final cycle of comments and minor changes even after the submission)

10.7.3   Presenting and commenting on findings and drawing conclusions

Table 10.3   Examples of data commentary and diverse functions

Function of findings or data commentary sections in research texts	Examples from case-study articles in Chapter 5
To locate or direct the reader to detailed information	Final consonant clusters in the data, along with the words in which they appear, together with their pronunciations, are listed in Appendix B (Osborne, 1996: 169)
	Table 10.1 presents the findings (Lennon, 1990: 409)
	The overall results are presented in Figure 1 (Saffran, Newport and Asin, 1996: 613)
To direct the reader's attention to significant information (*not* simply repeating data without any evaluative language)	As shown in Table 10.2, however, clusters which violate the sonority hierarchy are significantly less likely to be reduced than those which follow it (71.28 per cent to 95.27 per cent...) (Osborne, 1996: 173)
	Table 10.1 indicates that at Week 2 Dorothea's production contained more dysfluency markers...than did the other subjects (Lennon, 1990: 411)
	A single-sample t test (two-tailed) showed overall performance significantly different from chance: $t(11) - 6.78$, $p < 0.01$ (Saffran, Newport and Asin, 1996: 613)
To begin to draw conclusions relating directly to the data	In treating final /r/ as part of the syllabic nucleus, the subject's performance on the tapes is in line with Kahn's (1976: 150–2) classification of English /r/ as a glide rather than a sonorant consonant...(Osborne, 1996: 171)
	It would appear, in fact, that fluency improvements for Dorothea were concentrated on those areas that were relatively weak in Week 2, rather than occurring across the board (Lennon, 1990: 411)
	These data indicate that subjects confused words with part-words which resembled the ends of words more often than with part-words which resembled the beginnings of words (Saffran, Newport and Asin, 1996: 615)

10.7.4   Drawing conclusions

Table 10.4   **Features of conclusions**

Contains new ideas/information?	X
Contains repetition of main points of argument or of findings?	✓
Focuses on the best ideas you have had to 'sell' them to the reader?	✓
Gives a broad summary of all your points, whether stronger or weaker?	X
Links back clearly to the original research questions?	✓
Gives sense of how far the research questions were answered?	✓
Hides any problems and limitations of the research process?	X
Expresses the limitations of the research and possible further research?	✓
Gives a clear sense of finality to the research text?	✓

10.8   Other on-line resources

An excellent general web-site for the applied linguist is:
http://www.linguistlist.org/
From this it is possible to search through, or join, various discussion groups; for instance, that on discourse at:
http://www.linguistlist.org/subscribing/sub-discours.html or language and culture:
http://www.linguistlist.org/subscribing/sub-l-c.html
A good starting point for links on language teaching is at:
http://www2.rgu.ac.uk/~sim/cml/ling_res.htm
The Centre for Information on Language Teaching and Research (CILT) provides a forum and a 'virtual language centre' at:
http://www.linguanet.org.uk/
The Speech, Hearing and Language Research Centre of Macquarie University can be visited at:
http://www.shlrc.mq.edu.au/
There is an on-line bibliography of Ethnolinguistics and Conversation Analysis at:
http://www.pscw.uva.nl/emca/resource.htm
Resources on speaking in a business context are to be found at:
http://www.hio.ft.hanze.nl/thar/speaking.htm
A resource which provides on-line ideas for games and activities to generate speaking can be found at:
http://www2.ice.usp.ac.jp/wklinger/QA/cardgameshome.htm
General advice on teaching and learning speaking, as well as teaching resources can be found at:
http://eleaston.com/speaking.html

A highly useful site of tips, techniques and news can be found at:
http://www.everythingesl.net/
The Internet TESL Journal at:
http://www.aitech.ac.jp/~iteslj/ provides both research-based articles and
more teaching-oriented material
TESL-L is a very extensive resource and discussion grouping which
can be joined at:
http://www.hunter.cuny.edu/~tesl-l/ and has searchable archives
The on-line language teacher can be accessed via:
http://langue.hyper.chubu.ac.jp/jalt/pub/tlt/index.html
The Educational Resources Information Center (ERIC) is a highly
user-friendly searchable database found at:
http://ericir.syr.edu/Eric/index.shtml

Glossary

Adjacency pairs This is a term from discourse and, more generally, conversation analysis. Whereas theoretical linguists might be interested in isolated sentences, discourse and conversation analysts look at utterances in relation to each other. The term adjacency pairs relates to two consecutive utterances which are so strongly related to one another in the conversational structure of a language that one seems bizarre without the other. In standard British conversation examples might be a greeting–greeting pair ('Hi'–'Hi'; 'How are you doing?'–'Fine, thanks') or a thanking exchange ('Thanks'–'My pleasure'; 'Thanks a lot'–'Not at all').

Avoidance Avoidance is a term used in the assessment of language ability, for example in testing or in analysis of the range of forms used by a learner. A learner may be very accurate in their production, but be functioning within a limited range of forms. By contrast, another learner may make a significantly higher number of errors, but be functioning within a more complex range of structures. The technical description of what the former is doing is 'avoidance'.

Back channel A term from conversation analysis and discourse analysis. This refers to the verbal and non-verbal feedback which a listener gives to a speaker during an interaction (for example, 'Yes', 'Mmm' or 'I see').

Circumlocution Generally a circumlocution is an extended, long-winded or roundabout way of expressing an idea (perhaps in order to avoid a very explicit phrase which might cause offence). In applied linguistics the term crops up in the investigation of communication strategies in relation to a learner's ability to express an idea for which they do not know the word in their target language.

Discourse marker A word or phrase which is used by a speaker (or writer) to orient the listener in some way. The word or phrase has little meaning in its own right but provides a point of reference for the listener in relation to either the structure of the talk and topic ('Right', 'OK', 'Now') or the opinion of the speaker ('Yeah', 'Sure', 'Well').

Ellipsis A feature found in both speech and writing, but which has been studied less in relation to the former. A standard sentence contains certain grammatical elements which a 'full' rendering of the sentence would show. In English we expect perhaps a Subject + Verb + Object given a transitive verb. Other languages standardly omit the Subject element. However, when an element which you would normally expect is left out this process is called 'ellipsis'. Therefore, when a speaker says 'Ready yet?' in place of 'Are you ready yet?' and someone replies 'Coming!' instead of 'I'm coming' both are using ellipsis of subject and auxiliary verb. It is important for learners of spoken language to become able to use ellipsis naturally so that they do not sound overly formal or ponderous. However, this is much easier to teach in relation to the written form where the patterns are less complex. A real issue in relation to ellipsis in speech is how far any underlying full structure is clear and available for analysis.

Face This is an expression used both as a lay term and, more technically, in the field of pragmatics. The term 'to lose face' indicates that a person has lost esteem in the eyes of others. In most cultures a considerable amount of conversational exchange is devoted to ensuring that politeness conventions are met, and that an interlocutor does not feel uncomfortable. Facework is a term used to describe the sections of conversation where this most obviously takes place. For example, in British culture, speakers may ask about health or talk about the weather before developing a conversation further. If a particularly difficult or embarrassing topic has to be raised quite elaborate facework may be engaged in to assess the situation before the subject is broached. Different cultures have different attitudes to face, and facework is carried out via very different mechanisms (or 'realisations') in different languages.

Formulaic exchange/utterance One of the distinguishing characteristics of the human capacity for language, according to Noam Chomsky, is the level of creativity it allows. However, not all language is novel and completely distinctive. Many sections of conversational exchange are highly predictable, although these will vary from culture to culture and language to language. For example, the opening and closing of a conversation generally follows a pattern which speakers are hardly conscious of, but which, if breached, will cause confusion and mis-communication. In particular, the treatment of functions, such as offering food or drink (in your culture do you refuse, but expect to be offered a second time?) or giving/accepting compliments (do you automatically denigrate the object which has been admired?), tend to have strongly established patterns. These patterns are so conventional they are known as formulaic exchanges or utterances.

Interlocutor This is a more technical term for a language sender/receiver (a speaker/writer, listener/reader). It is a useful term because you do not have to specify the direction of message as the word contains a sense of two-way communication.

Intonation The aspect of the stream of speech which can be isolated in terms of pitch, combined with stress and speed, and which in many language is meaning bearing (for example, in British English the rise at the end of a yes/no question).

L1 First language

L2 Second language

Metalanguage This is language used to talk about language and language processes. When speakers engage in a standard conversation they do not normally comment on the process of the conversation or discuss the language in an abstract way. Two speakers may say to one another 'Morning', 'Morning' or 'Hi', 'How are you?' but they rarely think about this as a pair of 'greetings' or two 'openings' to a conversation, or an 'exchange' or an 'interaction', 'turn' or 'move'. All these ways of describing the speaker's language are examples of metalanguage.

Phonemics The study of the meaningful sound contrasts in a language. For example, although in English there are two different /l/ sounds depending on the position of the phoneme in a word (if you say the word 'little' you will hear both the 'light' /l/ at the start of the word and the 'dark' one at the end) they are not used to distinguish one word from another. In contrast the two 'th' sounds in English /Ø/ (**thin**) and /ð/ (**these**) are used to distinguish one word from another, for instance, teeth–teethe, wreath–wreathe.

Phonetics The study of the sounds of a language. In this science the focus is on the flow of sounds in relation to one another and their analysis through sound spectrography and phonetic symbols.

Phonology The study of the sound structure of a language especially in the context of changes to the sounds of words through time and/or the relations between the historical development of different languages.

Pragmatics In studying discourse analysis you will probably come across words like pragmatic and cultural and context quite a few times and may wonder what the difference is between 'discourse analysis' and 'pragmatics'. In the case of the former the focus is more strongly on the actual words, phrases and chunks of language produced and how these interrelate to make up typical patterns. In the case of the latter, the focus is more on the kinds of knowledge, beliefs or understandings which speakers have about the way they should behave in communication, and this is sometimes referred to as 'pragmatic knowledge'.

Prosody The parts of the stream of spoken language which carry meaning, but are beyond the confines of words and clauses, and are strictly sound based. Pitch, intonation, rhythm are all parts of the prosodic system of a language.

Service encounter A term from discourse analysis to describe spoken genres which revolve around trade and business service, such as encounters in banks, post offices or ticket offices.

Socio-linguistics The branch of linguistics which is particularly interested in the interaction between language use and social influences. Whereas a discourse analyst might be interested in patterns of interaction within a conversation, the socio-linguist is concerned with how the speech of an individual or group is affected by social, economic or geographic factors.

Speech recognition The process by which a computer or other non-human communication device understands and interacts with a human user.

Speech synthesis The process of imitating human speech via computer systems.

Speech therapy/pathology Speech which is produced with difficulty (for example, stammering), or, in a child, speech which is below the level expected for a particular stage in development may need the assistance of speech therapy. Speech pathology tends to be used for problems with the faculty of speech which are the result of accident, illness or other trauma.

Suprasegmental This is a term from phonetics. As well as vowel and consonant sounds in a language there are meaningful elements which occur simultaneously with them, such as pitch, stress and intonation. These are known as suprasegmentals because they function above or across the boundaries of the other elements which are studied.

T-Unit This stands for 'thought unit'. There are a number of different definitions of this, but the two main areas they have been used in are literacy/readability studies and the study of spoken genres. The concept is regarded as useful because it gets away from the sometimes difficult to define clause and sentence units. Within spoken analysis the rather loose definition of 'a group of words expressing one idea' is tightened by the use of intonation (downward in English) and slight pausing to mark the ends of a t-unit.

Text analysis This is the sister discipline of discourse analysis. Whereas the latter tends to be more interested in the spoken mode, text analysis, as the name suggests, is concerned with extended stretches of written language and how they cohere. Both disciplines share a common interest in patterns of language and relations between elements beyond the level of the clause.

Turn-taking The process by which speakers interact with one another. A large amount of work in discourse analysis is interested in how speakers know that they have a right to speak and precisely when.

References

Aarts, B. and Meyer, C. (Eds) (1995). *The Verb in Contemporary English: theory and description*. Cambridge: Cambridge University Press.

Auer, J. (1959). *An Introduction to Research in Speech*. New York: Harper and Brothers.

Bachman, L. F. (1990). *Fundamental Considerations in Language Testing*. Oxford: Oxford University Press.

Barzun, J. and Graff, H. F. (1992). *The Modern Researcher*. Orlando: Harcourt Brace Jovanovich.

Bastow, T. and Jones, C. (1994). *Talking in Pairs*. Oxford: Oxford University Press.

Benson, B. (1988). Universal preference for the open syllable as an independent process in interlanguage phonology. *Language Learning*. 38: 221–242.

Berg, T. (1997). The modality-specificity of linguistic representations: evidence from slips of the tongue and the pen. *Journal of Pragmatics*. 27(5): 671–697.

Berg, T. and Hassan, A. (1996). The unfolding of suprasegmental representations: a cross-linguistic perspective. *Journal of Linguistics*. 32: 291–324.

Biber, D. (1986). Spoken and written textual dimensions in English: resolving the contradictory findings. *Language*. 62: 384–414.

Biber, D. (1988). *Variation across Speech and Writing*. Cambridge: Cambridge University Press.

Biber, D. (1995). *Dimensions of Register Variation*. Cambridge: Cambridge University Press.

Biber, D., Johansson, S., Leech, G., Conrad, S. and Finegan, E. (1999). *Longman Grammar of Spoken and Written English*. Harlow: Longman.

Bourdin, B. and Fayol, M. (1996). Mode effects in a sentence production span task. *Cahiers de Psychologie Cognitive*. 15/3: 245–264.

Brazil, D. (1994). *Pronunciation for Advanced Learners of English*. Cambridge: Cambridge University Press.

Brazil, D. (1995). *A Grammar of Speech*. Oxford: Oxford University Press.

Bremer, K., Roberts, C., Vasseur, M. T., Simonot, M. and Broeder, P. (1996). *Achieving Understanding: discourse in intercultural encounters*. London: Longman.

Brown, G. and Yule, G. (1983). *Teaching the Spoken Language: an approach based on the analysis of conversational English*. Cambridge: Cambridge University Press.

Brown, H. D. (1994). *Teaching by Principles: an interactive approach to language pedagogy.* Englewood Cliffs, NJ: Prentice Hall Regents.

Brown, R. S. and Nation, P. (1997). Teaching speaking: suggestions for the classroom. *The Language Teacher Online.* 21/1.

Browning, G. (1985). What makes ESL students' speech sound unacceptable? CATESOL Occasional Papers. 11: 72–81.

Burns, A. and Joyce, H. (1997). *Focus on Speaking.* Sydney: National Center for English Language Teaching and Research, Macquarie University.

Burton, J. (1998). A cross-case analysis of teacher involvement in TESOL research. *TESOL Quarterly.* 32/3.

Butler, F. A., Eignor, D., Jones, S., McNamara, T. and Suomi, B. K. (2000). TOEFL 2000 speaking framework: a working paper. *TOEFL Monograph Series* 20. Princeton, NJ: Educational Testing Service.

Bygate, M. (1987). *Speaking.* Oxford: Oxford University Press.

Bygate, M. (1999). Quality of language and purpose of task: patterns of learners' language on two oral communication tasks. *Language Teaching Research.* 3/3: 185–214.

Byrne, D. (1986). *Teaching Oral English.* Harlow: Longman.

Call, M. E. and Sotillo, S. M. (1995). Is talk cheap? The role of conversation in the acquisition of language. *Hispania.* 78(1): 114–121.

Carter, R., Hughes, R. and McCarthy, M. (2000). *Exploring Grammar in Context.* Cambridge: Cambridge University Press.

Carter, R. and McCarthy, M. (1995). Grammar and the spoken language. *Applied Linguistics.* 16(2): 141–158.

Carter, R. and McCarthy, M. (1997). *Exploring Spoken English.* Cambridge: Cambridge University Press.

Carter, R. and McCarthy, M. (forthcoming). *The Cambridge Advanced Grammar of English.* Cambridge: Cambridge University Press.

Chafe, W. and Danielewicz, J. (1987). Properties of spoken and written language. In R. Horowitz and S. J. Samuels (Eds), *Comprehending Oral and Written Language.* San Diego, CA: Academic Press, pp. 83–113.

Chomsky, N. (1965). *Aspects of the Theory of Syntax.* Cambridge, MA: MIT Press.

Clancier, A. (1998). La parole et l'écriture. *Revue Française de Psychanalyse.* 62(3): 931–935.

Clark, H. H. and Wasow, T. (1998). Repeating words in spontaneous speech. *Cognitive Psychology.* 37(3): 201–242.

Clarke, M. A. (1994). The dysfunctions of the theory/practice discourse. *TESOL Quarterly.* 28(1).

Cook, V. and Newson, M. (1996). *Chomsky's Universal Grammar: an introduction.* Oxford: Blackwell.

Croisilie, B., Brabant, M. J., Carmol, T., Lepage, Y., Aimard, G. and Trillet, M. (1996). Comparison between oral and written spelling in Alzheimer's disease. *Brain and Language.* 54(3): 361–387.

Cross, D. (1992). *A Practical Handbook of Language Teaching.* Hemel Hempstead: Prentice Hall.

Cunningham, S. and Moor, P. (1992). *Everyday Listening and Speaking.* Oxford: Oxford University Press.

Daly-Jones, O., Monk, A., Frolich, D., Geelhoed, E. and Loughran, S. (1997). Multimodal messages: the pen and voice opportunity. *Interacting with Computers*. 9: 1–25.

De Beaugrande, R. (1994). Speech and writing in theory and in data. In S. Cmejrkova, F. Danes and E. Havlova (Eds), *Writing vs Speaking: language, text, discourse, communication*. Tubingen: Gunter Narr Verlag, pp. 23–46.

De Gelder, B. and Vroomen, J. (1997). Modality effects in immediate recall of verbal and non-verbal information. *The European Journal of Cognitive Psychology*. 9: 97–110.

De Kerkehove, D. (1986). Alphabetic literacy and brain processes. *Visible Language*. 20(3): 274–293.

Deacon, T. W. (1996). Prefrontal cortex and symbol learning: why a brain capable of language evolved only once. In B. M. Velichkovsky and D. M. Rumbaugh (Eds), *Communicating Meaning: the evolution and development of language*. Mahwah, NJ: Lawrence Erlbaum Associates.

DePoy, E. and Gitlin L. N. (1993). *Introduction to Research: strategies for health and human services*. St Louis: Mosby-Year Book Inc.

Derwing, T. M., Monro, M. J. and Wiebe, G. (1998). Evidence in favor of a broad framework for pronunciation instruction. *Language Learning*. 48(3): 393–410.

Dörnyei, Z. (1995). On the teachability of communication strategies. *Tesol Quarterly*. 29(1): 55–84.

Dornyei, Z. and Kormos, J. (2000). The role of individual and social variables in oral task performance. *Language Teaching Research*. 4(3): 275–300.

Dörnyei, Z. and Scott, M. L. (1997). Communication strategies in a second language: definitions and taxonomies. *Language Learning*. 47(1): 173–210.

Douglas, D. (1997). Testing speaking ability in academic contexts: theoretical considerations. *TOEFL Monograph Series*. Princeton, NJ: Educational Testing Services.

Douglas, D. (2000). *Assessing Languages for Specific Purposes*. Cambridge: Cambridge University Press.

Eckman, F. (1986). The reduction of word-final consonant clusters in interlanguage. In A. James and J. Leather (Eds), *Sound Patterns in Second Language Acquisition*. Dortrecht: Foris.

Eisenstein, M. and Bodman, J. (1993). Expressing gratitude in American English. In G. Kasper and S. Blum-Kulka (Eds), *Interlanguage Pragmatics*. New York: Oxford University Press.

Ervin-Tripp, S. (1993). Conversational discourse. In J. Berko Gleason and N. Berstein Ratner (Eds), *Psycholinguistics*. Orlando, FL: Harcourt, Brace, Jovanovich, pp. 238–270.

Florez, M. C. (1999). Improving adult English language learners' speaking skills. Report for National Clearinghouse for ESL Literacy Education (NCLE). Washington, DC: National Clearinghouse for ESL Literacy Education.

Forsey, J., Kay-Raining-Bird, E. and Bedrosian, J. (1996). The effects of typed and spoken modality combinations on the language performance of adults with autism. *Journal of Autism and Developmental Disorders*. 26(6): 643–649.

Geddes, M. and Sturtridge, G. (1992). *Elementary Conversation*. London: Macmillan.

Gimson, A. C. (1978). *A Practical Course of English Pronunciation*. London: Edward Arnold.

Glisan, E. W. and Drescher, V. (1993). Textbook grammar: does it reflect native speaker speech? *Modern Language Journal*. 77(1): 23–33.

Goodwin, C. (1981). *Conversational Organisation: interaction between speakers and hearers.* New York: Academic Press.

Goody, J. (1977). *The Domestication of the Savage Mind.* Cambridge: Cambridge University Press.

Goody, J. (1987). *The Interface between the Written and the Oral.* Cambridge: Cambridge University Press.

Goody, J. (2000). *The Power of the Written Tradition.* Washington, DC: Smithsonian Institute.

Grabowski, J. (1996). Writing and speaking: common grounds and differences toward a regulation theory of written language production. In M. C. Levy *et al.* (Eds), *The Science of Writing: theories, methods, individual differences and applications.* Mahwah, NJ: Lawrence Erlbaum Associates.

Griffiths, R. (1990). Speech rate and NNS comprehension: a preliminary study in time–benefit analysis. *Language Learning.* 40(3): 311–336.

Gundel, J., Hedberg, N. and Zacharski, R. (1993). Cognitive status and the form of referring expressions. *Language.* 69(2): 274–307.

Gunn, B. (trans.) (1918). *The Instruction of Ptah-ho-tep and the Instruction of Kegemni: the oldest books in the world.* London: John Murray.

Halliday, M. A. K. (1989). *Spoken and Written Language.* Oxford: Oxford University Press.

Hammerly, H. (1991). *Fluency and Accuracy: towards balance in language teaching and learning.* Bristol, PA: Multilingual Matters Ltd.

Hargreaves, R. and Fletcher, M. (1979). *Making Polite Noises.* London: Evans.

Harmer, Jeremy (2001). *The Practice of English Language Teaching.* Harlow: Longman.

Harris, W. V. (1989). *Ancient Literacy.* Cambridge: Cambridge University Press.

Hatch, E. (1992). *Discourse and Language Education.* Cambridge: Cambridge University Press.

Hawkins, E. (1983). *Spoken and Written Language.* Melbourne: Cambridge University Press.

Haynes, L. A. (1992). The development of speaking/writing variability in narratives of non-native English speakers. *Issues in Applied Linguistics.* 3(1): 43–67.

Herrmann, T. (1986). *Speech and Situation: a psychological conception of situated speaking.* Berlin: Springer-Verlag.

Hoey, M. (1991). Some properties of spoken discourses. In R. Bowers and C. Brumfit (Eds), *Applied Linguistics and English Language Teaching.* Oxford: Modern English Publications in association with The British Council.

Holliday, A. (2001). *Doing and Writing Qualitiative Research.* Thousand Oaks, CA: Sage Publications.

Holmes, J. (1988). Doubt and certainty in ESL textbooks. *Applied Linguistics.* 9.

Howatt, A. P. R. (1985). *A History of English Language Teaching.* Oxford: Oxford University Press.

Hughes, R. (1996). *English in Speech and Writing: investigating language and literature.* London: Routledge.

Hughes, R. and McCarthy, M. (1998). Sentence grammar and discourse grammar. *TESOL Quarterly.* 32(2): 263–287.

Hutchinson, T. and Torres, E. (1994). The textbook as an agent of change. *ELT Journal.* 48(4).

Hyland, K. (2002). *Teaching and Researching Writing.* Harlow: Longman.

IELTS (2001). *IELTS: International English Language Testing System Handbook* (July).

Iwashita, N., McNamara, T. and Elder, C. (2001). Can we predict task difficulty in an oral proficiency test? Exploring the potential of an information-processing approach to task design. *Language Learning*. 51(3): 401–436.

Janssen, D., van Waes, L. and van den Bergh, H. (1996). Effects of thinking aloud on writing processes. In C. M. Levy and S. Ransdall (Eds), *The Science of Writing, Theories, Methods, Individual Differences and Applications*. Mahwah, NJ: Lawrence Erbaoum Associates.

Johns, T. (1991). From printout to handout: grammar and vocabulary learning in the context of data-driven learning. *English Language Research Journal*. 4: 27–45. University of Birmingham.

Johnson, M. and Tyler, A. (1998). Re-analysing the OPI: how much does it look like natural conversation? In R. Young and A. Weiyn He (Eds), *Talking and Testing: Discourse approaches to the assessment of oral proficiency*. Studies in Bilingualism. 14: 27–51. Amsterdam and Philadelphia: John Benjamins Publishing Company.

Jones, E. E. and Frawley, W. (1967). *Foundations of Social Psychology*. New York: Wiley.

Jones, I. (1998). The effect of computer-generated spoken feedback on kindergarten students' written narratives. *Journal of Computing in Childhood Education*. 9(1): 43–56.

Keller, E. and Warner, S. T. (1988). *Conversation Gambits*. Hove: Language Teaching Publications.

Kerlinger, F. N. (1973). *Foundations of Behavioural Research*. New York: Holt, Rinehart and Winston.

Kinoshita, S. (1998). The role of phonology in reading Japanese: or why I don't hear myself when reading Japanese. *Reading and Writing* 10(3–5): 439–455.

Klein, W. and Purdue, C. (Eds) (1992). *Utterance Structure: developing grammars again* Amsterdam and Philadelphia, PA: John Benjamins Publishing Co.

Knowles, G. (1990). The use of spoken and written corpora in the teaching of language and linguistics. *Literary and Linguistic Computing*. 5: 45–48.

Kasper, G. and Blum-Kulka, S. (1993). *Interlanguage Pragmatics*. New York: Oxford University Press.

Krashen, S. D. (1982). *Principles and Practice in Second Language Acquisition*. Oxford: Pergamon.

Labov, W. (1973). *Sociolinguistic Patterns*. Pennsylvania: University of Pennsylvania Press.

Lazaraton, A. (1995). Qualitative research in applied linguistics: a progress report. *TESOL Quarterly*. 29(3): 445–472.

Leech, G. (2000). Grammars of spoken English: new outcomes of corpus-oriented research. *Language Learning*. 50(4): 675–724.

Lennon, P. (1990). Investigating fluency in EFL: a quantitative approach. *Language Learning*. 40(3): 387–417.

Levelt, W. J. M. (1989). *Speaking: from intention to articulation*. Cambridge, MA and London, England: The MIT Press.

Lewis, M. (1982). *Partners 3: more demanding pair work practices*. Hove: Language Teaching Publications.

Liberman, A. M. (1997). How theories of speech affect research in reading and writing. In Benita A. Blachman (Ed.). *Foundations of Reading Acquisition and Dyslexia*. Mahwah, NJ: Lawrence Erlbaum Associates.

Liberman, A. M. (1998). When theories of speech meet the real world. *Journal of Psycholinguistic Research*. 27(2): 111–122.

Ling, L. E. and Grabe, E. (1999). A contrastive study of prosody and lexical stress placement in Singapore English and British English. *Language and Speech*. 42(1): 39–56.

Loveday, L. (1982). *The Sociolinguistics of Learning and Using a Non-native Language*. Oxford: Pergamon.

Lynch, T. (2001). Seeing what they meant: transcribing as a route to noticing. *ELT Journal*. 55(2): 124–132.

Lynch, T. and Anderson, K. (1992). *Study Speaking: a course in spoken English for academic purposes*. Cambridge: Cambridge University Press.

Mackenzie, C. (2000). Adult spoken discourse: the influences of age and education. *International Journal of Language and Communication Disorders*. 35(2): 269–285.

Mason, L. (1998). Sharing cognition to construct scientific knowledge in school context: the role of oral and written discourse. *Instructional Science*. 26(5): 359–389.

McCarthy, M. (1991). *Discourse Analysis for Language Teachers*. Cambridge: Cambridge University Press.

McCarthy, M. (1998). *Spoken Language and Applied Linguistics*. Cambridge: Cambridge University Press..

McCarthy, M. and Carter, R. (1994). *Language as Discourse: perspectives for language teaching*. Harlow: Longman.

McCarthy, M. and Carter, R. (forthcoming). Ten criteria for spoken grammar. In E. Hinkel and S. S. Fotos (Eds), *New Perspectives on Grammar Teaching in Second Language Classrooms*. New Jersey: Lawrence Erlbaum.

McDonough, J. and Shaw, C. (1993). *Materials and Methods in ELT: a teacher's guide*. Oxford: Blackwell.

McKay, S. L. and Hornberger, N. (Eds) (1996). *Sociolinguistics and Language Teaching*. Cambridge: Cambridge University Press.

Meyer, C. F. (1995). Coordination ellipsis in spoken and written American English. *Language Sciences*. 17: 241–269.

Miceli, G. and Capasso, R. (1997). Semantic errors as neuropsychological evidence for the independence and the interaction of orthographic and phonological word forms. *Language and Cognitive Processes*. 12(5 and 6): 733–764.

Miller, P. H., Pullem, G. K. and Zwicky, A. M. (1997). The principle of phonology-free syntax: four apparent counter examples from French. *Journal of Linguistics*. 33: 67–90.

Murphey, T. (2001). Exploring conversational shadowing. *Language Teaching Research*. 5(2): 128–155.

Nelson, G. (1997). Cleft constructions in spoken and written English. *Journal of English Linguistics*. 25: 340–348.

Nelson, G. L, Mahmood, A. and Nichols, E. (1996). Arabic and English compliment responses: potential for pragmatic failure. *Applied Linguistics*. 17(4): 411–432.

Nolasco, R. and Arthur, L. (1987). *Conversation*. Oxford: Oxford University Press.

Nunan, D. (1992). *Research Methods in Language Learning*. New York: Cambridge University Press.

Olson, D. (1996a). Towards a psychology of literacy: on the relations between speech and writing. *Cognition*. 60(1): 83–104.

Olson, D. (1996b). *The World on Paper*. Cambridge: Cambridge University Press.

Olson, D. and Torrance, N. (Eds) (1991). *Literacy and Orality*. Cambridge: Cambridge University Press.

O'Loughlin, K. (2001). *The Equivalence of Direct and Semi-Direct Speaking Tests.* Cambridge: Cambridge University Press.

O'Malley, J. M. and Valdez Pierce, L. (1996). *Authentic Assessment for English Language Learners: practical approaches for teachers.* New York: Addison Wesley.

Ong, W. J. (1971). *Rhetoric, Romance and Technology.* Ithaca and London: Cornell University Press.

Ong, W. J. (1982). *Orality and Literacy: the technologizing of the word.* London: Methuen.

Osborne, A. G. (1996). Final cluster reduction in English L2 speech: a case study of a Vietnamese speaker. *Applied Linguistics.* 17(2): 164–181.

Pennington, M. C. (1989). Teaching pronunciation from the top down. *RELC Journal: A Journal of Language Teaching and Research in Southeast Asia.* 20(1): 20–38.

Pennington, M. C. (1996). *Phonology in Language Teaching.* London: Longman.

Pennington, M. C. (forthcomng). *Teaching and Researching Pronunciation.* London: Longman.

Pennington, M. C. and Richards, J. C. (1986). Pronunciation revisited. *TESOL Quarterly.* 20(2): 207–235.

Pica, T., Lincoln-Porter, F., Panino, D. and Linell, J. (1996). Language learners' interaction. how does it address the input, output and feedback needs of language learners? *Tesol Quarterly.* 30(1): 59–84.

Pound, C. (1996). Writing remediation using preserved oral spelling: a case for separate output buffers. *Aphasiology.* 10(3): 283–296.

Rapp, B. and Caramazza, A. (1997). The modality-specific organization of grammatical categories: evidence from impaired spoken and written sentence production. *Brain and Language.* 56: 248–286.

Reece, J. E. and Cumming, G. (1996). Evaluating speech-based composition methods: planning, dictation, and the listening word processor. In M. C. Levy and S. Ransdell (Eds), *The Science of Writing: theories, methods, individual differences and applications.* Mahwah, NJ: Lawrence Erlbaum Associates.

Riggenbach, H. (1998). Evaluating learner interactional skills: conversation at the micro level. In R. Young and A. Weiyun He (Eds), *Talking and Testing: discourse approaches to the assessment of oral proficiency.* Studies in Bilingualism, 14. Amsterdam and Philadelphia: John Benjamins Publishing Company, pp. 53–67.

Rignall, M. and Furneaux, C. (1997). *Speaking* (English for Academic study series). Hemel Hempstead: Prentice Hall.

Rivers, W. M. and Temperley, M. S. (1978). *A Practical Guide to the Teaching of English as a Second or Foreign Language.* New York: Oxford University Press.

Rose, K. R. and Kasper, G. (2001). *Pragmatics in Language Teaching.* Cambridge: Cambridge University Press.

Rost, M. (2002). *Teaching and Researching Listening.* Harlow: Longman.

Saffran, J. R., Newport, E. L. and Asin, R. N. (1996). Word segmentation: the role of distributional cues. *Journal of Memory and Language.* 35: 606–621.

Sánchez Macarro, A. and Carter, R. (Eds) (1998). *Linguistic Choice Across Genres: variation in spoken and written English.* Amsterdam: John Benjamins.

Sarwark, S., Smith, J., MacCullam, R. and Cascallar, E. C. (1995). *A Study of Characteristics of the SPEAK Test.* RR94–47. Princeton, NJ: Educational Testing Service.

Scheerer, E. (1996). Orality, literacy and cognitive modeling. In B. M. Velichkovsky and D. M. Rumbaugh (Eds), *Communicating Meaning: the evolution and development of language.* Mahwah, NJ: Lawrence Erlbaum Associates.

Schegloff, E. A. (1968). Sequencing in conversational openings. *American Anthropologist*. 70: 1075–1095.

Schegloff, E. A. (1979). Identification and recognition in telephone conversation openings. In G. Psathas (Ed.), *Everyday Language: studies in ethnomethodology*. New York: Irvington, pp. 23–78.

Schegloff, E. A. (1981). Discourse as an interactional achievement: some uses of 'uh huh' and other things that come between sentences. In D. Tannen (Ed.), *Analysing Discourse: text and talk*. Washington DC: Georgetown University Press.

Scollon, R. and Wong-Scollon, S. (1991). Topic confusion in English–Asian discourse. *World Englishes*. 10(2): 113–125.

Shelton, J. R. and Weinrich, M. (1997). Further evidence of a dissociation between output from phonological and orthographic lexicons: a case study. *Cognitive Neuropsychology*. 14(1): 105–129.

Sheridan, T. (1791). *A Rhetorical Grammar of the English Language* (reprinted 1969). Menston, England: The Scholar Press.

Shin, D. H. (1989). Effect of formal vs. informal environments and Krashen's Monitor Model. Unpublished Master's thesis, University of Birmingham, Birmingham, West Midlands.

Sinclair, J. and Coulthard, M. (1975). *Towards an Analysis of Discourse: the English used by teachers and pupils*. London: Oxford University Press.

Skehan, P. (1998). *A Cognitive Approach to Language Learning*. Oxford: Oxford University Press.

Skinner, B. F. (1978). *Reflections on Behaviourism [sic] and Society*. London: Prentice Hall.

Sperling, M. (1996). Revisiting the writing–speaking connection: challenges for research on writing and writing instruction. *Review of Educational Research*. 66(1): 53–86.

Stenström, A-B. (1990). Lexical items peculiar to spoken discourse. In J. Svartvik (Ed.), *The London-Lund Corpus of Spoken English: description and research*. Lund Studies in English 82. Lund: Lund University Press, pp. 137–176.

Svartvik, J. (Ed.) (1990). *The London–Lund Corpus of Spoken English: description and research*. Lund Studies in English 82. Lund: Lund University Press.

Svartvik, J. (1991). What can real spoken data teach teachers of English? In J. E. Alatis (Ed.), *Georgetown University Round Table on Languages and Linguistics 1991*. Washington, DC: Georgetown University Press, pp. 555–566.

Takehashi, T. and Beebe, L. M. (1993). Cross-linguistic influence in the speech act of correction. In G. Kasper and S. Blum-Kulka (Eds), *Interlanguage Pragmatics*. New York: Oxford University Press.

Tavassoli, N. T. (1998). Language in multimedia: interaction of spoken and written information. *Journal of Consumer Research*. 25(1): 26–37.

Towell, R., Hawkins, R. and Bazergui, N. (1996). The development of fluency in advanced learners of French. *Applied Linguistics*. 17(1): 84–119.

Tribble, C. and Jones, G. (1990). *Concordances in the Classroom: a resource book for teachers*. Harlow: Longman.

Trudgill, P. (2000). *Sociolinguistics*. London: Penguin.

Tsui, A. B. M. (1994). *English Conversation*. Oxford: Oxford University Press.

Tyler, A. E., Jeffries, A. A. and Davies, C. E. (1988). The effect of discourse structuring devices on listener perceptions of coherence in non-native university teacher's spoken discourse. *World Englishes*. 7(2): 101–110.

UCLES (2000a). *Certificates in English Language Skills (CELS): specifications and sample papers.* Cambridge: University of Cambridge Local Examinations Syndicate.

UCLES (2000b). *Certificate of Proficeincy in English: revised CPE specifications and sample papers.* Cambridge: University of Cambridge Local Examinations Syndicate.

Underhill, N. (1987). *Testing Spoken Language: a handbook of oral testing techniques.* Cambridge: Cambridge University Press.

Ur, P. (1996). *A Course in Language Teaching: practice and theory.* Cambridge: Cambridge University Press.

Vacheck, J. (1966). Some remarks on writing and phonetic transcription. In E. Hamp, F. Householder and R. Austerlitz (Eds), *Readings in Linguistics.* 2. Chicago: University of Chicago Press.

Vachek, J. (1973). *Written Language: general problems and problems of English.* The Hague: Mouton.

Vieiro, P. and García-Madruga, J. A. (1997). An analysis of story comprehension through spoken and written summaries in school-age children. *Reading and Writing: An interdisciplinary iournal.* 9: 41–53.

Wallwork, A. (1997). *Discussions A–Z, Intermediate: a resource book of speaking activities* Cambridge: Cambridge University Press.

Wardhaugh, R. (1992). *An Introduction to Sociolinguistics.* Cambridge, MA: Blackwell.

Watson-Gegeo, K. A. (1988). Ethnography in ESL: Defining the essentials. *TESOL Quarterly.* 22: 575–592.

White, R. (1997). Back chanelling, repair, parsing and private speech. *Applied Linguistics.* 18(3): 314–344.

Wilson, P. (2000). *Mind the Gap: ellipsis and stylistic variation in spoken and written English.* Harlow: Longman.

Wingate, J. (1993). *Getting Beginners to Talk.* Hemel Hempstead: Prentice Hall International English Language Teaching.

Wong, J. (2000). Repetition in conversation: a look at 'first and second sayings'. *Research on Language and Social Interaction.* 33(4): 407–424.

Wood, L. A. and Kroger, R. O. (2000). *Doing Discourse Analysis.* Thousand Oaks, CA: Sage Publications.

Woolfson, N. (1989). *Perspectives: sociolinguistics and TESOL.* New York: Harper Row.

Young, R. and Weiyun He, A. (1998). *Talking and Testing: discourse approaches to the assessment of oral proficiency.* Studies in Bilingualism, 14. Amsterdam and Philadelphia: John Benjamins Publishing Company.

Yungzhong, L. (1985). Writing versus speech in foreign language teaching. *Wai Guo Yu.* 3(37): 12–15.

Zobl, H. (1984). The wave model of linguistic change and the naturalness of interlanguage. *Studies in Second Language Acquisition.* 6(2): 160–185.

Zuengler, J. (1987). Effects of 'Expertise' in interactions between native and non-native speakers. *Language and Communication.* 7(2): 123–137.

Index

accents 68–70
action research 31, 32
Acts of Parliament 14
age, speech production and 146–8
Alexander, Louis 100
Alzheimer's patients 124
applied linguistics 49, 122
arguments and counter-arguments 52
Aristotle: *Rhetoric* 20
aspects of production 9, 10
aural channel 12
authentic speech 79–82
autism 125
avoidance/replacement 93

Beaugrande, Robert de 33
behaviourism 17
brain
  grammar, modality and 104–7
  modality 124–5
  speech, writing and 124
breakdown of discourse competence 81
broad sense fluency 112
Byrne, D., on oral fluency 67

call–answer 94–7
Cambridge Advanced Examinations (CAE) 84
Cambridge Proficiency Examinations (CPE) 84, 86
CANCODE (Cambridge and Nottingham Corpus of Discourse in English) 99–100
Certificate of Proficiency in English (CPE) 87
Certificates in English Language Skills (CELS) 84, 85–6, 88
Certificates in Communicative use of English (CCSE) 84
channel 12
children, mastering of language by 15–16, 35
Chomsky, Noam 15–16, 23, 29
Cicero 20–1
  De Oratore 21

circumlocution 93
classical research paradigms 27–8
clauses 40
clusters 109
cognitive linguistics 18
communication strategies 91
communicative approaches 23–4, 35, 48
competence 15, 16, 17
computational linguistics 34
conversation analysis 17, 18, 34, 38, 50
conversational genre 100
conversational patterns
  non-transferability across cultures 135
conversational shadowing 149–51
conversations
  language within 13
  preconceptions 76
  starting and finishing 54
Corax of Syracuse 20
corpora/corpus 7, 8, 30
  approach to grammar 31
  spoken 18, 40, 173
corpus analysis tools 30
corpus informed approach 99–101
corpus linguistics 8, 34, 40, 169–70
counter-arguments 52
critical linguistics 34
cross-cultural studies 168–98
cross-linguistic approaches 108
cycle of research 175–6

data commentary 176–7
databases 172–3
debate, oratical devices in 14
deficiency models of spoken discourse 149
Demosthenes 20
DePoy, E. and Gitlin, L. N.
  on action research 32
  on naturalistic enquiry 33
dialogues 48
direct methods 22–3
disagreeing 57

discourse ability 94–7
discourse analysis 17, 18, 34, 36–9, 50
discourse markers 37
discourse, spoken
    creating research project on 136–8
    implications of, on teaching speech 134–6
    sources of inspiration for research into
        138–41
        developments in the profession 139–40
        personal experience of the profession
            138–9
        published research and theory 140–1
        social or pragmatic issues 140
    theoretically oriented work 97–9
discussion 57
disputation 20
distribution cues to word boundaries 114–17
Dörnyei, Zoltan, on communication strategies
    90–4
Douglas, D.
    on discourse ability 94
    on integrated vs discrete skills testing 83–4
    on natural spoken discourse under test
        conditions 80
    on oral tests 74, 76

EAP 55
education, speech production and 146–8
Educational Testing Service 79
Egypt, Ancient 19–20
Eisenstein, M. and Bodman, J., on cross-
    cultural norms of thanking 139
elicitation techniques 48
ellipsis 40, 100
empiricism in linguistics 16
ESP 57
ethnographic studies 32, 39, 168–9
ethno-linguistics 49
exchanges 37

faculty of speech 15
final cluster reduction 110–11
First Certificate Examinations (FCE) 84
Florez, M. C., on good speakers 71
fluency 41–2, 67–70
    inter-lingual study 109–11
    quantitative approach 111–14
    research into 108–17
form movement 24
formulaic exchanges 37
functional or systemic linguistics 34, 122

Goodwin, C. on speech data 28
grammar 21, 39–41
    brain function and modality 104–7
    corpus-based approaches to 31
    generation 15
grammar of speech 6, 29, 30, 100

grammar translation methods 22, 23
Greece, Ancient 20

Halliday, M. A. K. 122
Hammerly, Hector, on communicative
    approach in relation to accuracy 68
historical perspectives 19–24
Hoey, M., on the spoken discourse 138
Howatt, A. P. R., on eighteenth-century
    speech 22
human–computer interaction 125
human–machine speech 170

idiolect 64
IETLS (International English Language
    Testing System) 84, 86–7
indirect speech 100
information-processing approach 156
innate cognitive model of language 16
innovation in language 15
input hypothesis 134
interactive writing instruction 127
interactivity 78–9
intonation resources, on-line 174

Johnson, M. and Tyler, A.
    on conversation 76
    on Oral Proficiency interview 143–5

Krashen, Stephen 24

language
    in action 13, 100
    awareness 24, 134
    faculty 15
    innovation in 15
    ornamentation 21
    primary form (speech) 12, 13, 14
    second 8–9
language proficiency
    test 73–6
    versus speaking proficiency 76–8
language teaching syllabus, handbooks for
    47–9
Lazaraton, A. 32
learning-acquisition hypothesis 134
left dislocation 100
legal tasks 14–15
Lennon, P., on fluency 69, 111–14
Levelt, W. J. M.: Speaking: from intention to
    articulation 31
Liberman, A. M.
    on the biological basis of speech 104
    on spoken discourse 97–9
library resources, traditional 171–2
listening 12, 36, 53
logic 21
love-making, language of 59

Mackenzie, C., on age, education and speech production 146–8
McDonough, J. and Shaw, C., on status of speech 120
memory
  influence of speech on 122–3
  modality, processing and 125–6
mini-corpus 100, 101
mode
  differences between 158–63
  evidence of modal brain 124–5
  processing, memory and 125–6
  relative processing demands of speech and writing 160–3
  role in teaching writing skills 158–60
mode-based research 120–1
morphology 34
Murphey, T., on conversational shadowing 149–51

narrative 100, 126
narrow sense fluency 112
natural methods 22–3
naturalist research 33
neuro-linguistics 18, 34, 99, 104, 169
Nunan, D. 32

oral channel 12–13
oral interaction, projects on 143–8
Oral Proficiency Interview (OPI) 143–5
oral task difficulty, projects on 153–8
oral testing 73–6
  authentic conditions for 79–82
  comparison of test paradigms 84–6
  context and purpose 82
  integrated vs discrete skills testing 83–4
  spoken genres and 82–3
oratory 20
ornamentation, language 21
orthography 124
Osborne, Andrea, on clusters 109–11
Oxford EFL examinations 84

pair parts 37
papyrus 19–20
participatory action research (PAR) 32
pauses/fillers 93, 114
pedagogy of spoken word 19
performance 15, 17
persuasion 19, 20
philosophical logic 28
phonemes 69, 70
phonemic chart 70
phones 69, 70
phonetics 34
phonology 34, 124, 128
phrase box 51
Plato 20

position paper 97–8
pragmatics 49
prepositions 9
processing conditions 48
production
  aspects of 9, 10
  errors 18
pronunciation 39, 41–2, 67–70
  inter-lingual study 109–11
  on-line services 174
  research into 108–17
psychoanalysis 125
psycholinguistics 31, 34, 125, 169

questioning 57
Quintilian 20
  Instituto Oratore 21

Rapp, B. and Caramazza, A. on brain function and language 104–7
rationalist model 16, 17
real-time processing constraints 136
record keeping 14
Reform Movement 22
reinforcement 100
repetition in conversation 151–3
research questions 174–5
resources 171–9
rhetoric 19, 20
Riggenbach, H.
  on breakdown of discourse competence 81
  on preconceptions about speech 78
Roman civilisation 20–1

Saffran, J. R., Newport, E. L. and Asin, R. N. on word segmentation 114–17
Scollon, R. and Wong-Scollon, S., summons–answer model 94–7
second language
  acquisition 34, 35–6, 39
  speech/writing dichotomy 128–9
secondary form (writing) 12, 13, 14
semantics 34
seminar skills 57, 58
service encounter 100
skill of speaking 6–9
Skinner, B. F. 17
social aspects 9, 11
socio-linguistics 34, 49
Sophists 20
sound archives 172–3
SPEAK test (Speaking Proficiency English Assessment Kit) 79, 81
speaker errors 41
speech data, attitudes to 28–33
speech errors 39
speech recognition resources 174
speech/writing dichotomy 126–9

speech/writing variability 101–4
Sperling, M., in the influence of speech on writing 126–9
spoken data in models of grammar 63
spoken grammar
  attitudes to 61–2
  descriptive models in teaching materials 65–6
  ideology of 63–4
  idiolect 65
  standardisation 64–5
  teaching 61–7
standardisation of grammar 64–5
status of speech 120–1
  in applied linguistics 35–6
  theoretical orientations on 121–3
summons–answer model 94–7
Swan, Michael 100
syntax 34
systemic or functional linguistics 34, 122

tail slot 100
talking-to-learn 128
task-based learning 24
temporal component of fluency 113
tenses 40
Test of Spoken English (TSE) 78, 79
text-to-speech resources 174
thanking, cross-cultural norms 139
TOEFL 81, 84, 85
topical information 100
total physical response (TSR) approaches 22–3
transactions 37
transformational grammar 23, 34
transitional probability 115, 116
turn relevance point (TRP) 37
Tyler, A. E., Jeffries, A. A. and Davies, C. E., on spoken academic discourse 138

Underhill, N., on oral tests 73–4
uniquely special qualities of speech 62

University of Cambridge Local Examinations Syndicate (UCLES) 84
  Cambridge Advanced Examinations (CAE) 84
  Cambridge Proficiency Examinations (CPE) 84, 86
  Certificates in English Language Skills (CELS) 84, 85–6, 88
  Certificates in Communicative use of English (CCSE) 84
  First Certificate Examinations (FCE) 84
  Main Suite examinations 84
Ur, P. 48
  on accents 68

vocabulary 39–41
vocabulary choices 12, 13
vocal dysfluency marker component 113
vocal pattern 35
voice quality 35

Watson-Gegeo, K. A. 32
Widdowson, Henry 24
Wong, Jean, on repetition 151–3
word
  boundaries 114–16
  definition 115
writing 7
  cf. speech 9
  influence of speech on 126–9
  influence on our view of speech 121
  on papyrus 19–20
  processing demands of 160–3
  role of speech in teaching 158–60
  transferability of speech into 14
  vocabulary choices 12

Yunzhong, L., on the valuing of speech in teaching 133

Zeno of Elea 20